ISBN-13: 978-0-9885855-0-8
BISAC CODE: 0CC019000

This publication is designed to provide accurate and authoritative information in regard to the subject matter covered. It is sold with the understanding that the publisher is not engaged in rendering legal, accounting, or other professional service. If legal advice or other expert assistance is required, the services of a competent professional person should be sought. – *From a Declaration of Principles Jointly Adopted by a Committee of the American Bar Association and a Committee of Publishers and Associations.*

All brand names and product names used in this book are trademarks, registered trademarks or trade names of their respective holders.

TVGuestpert Publishing is not associated with any product or vendor in this book.

TVGuestpert Publishing and the TVG logo are trademarks of Jacquie Jordan Inc.

TVGuestpert & TVGuestpert Publishing are visionary media companies that seek to educate, enlighten, and entertain the masses with the highest level of integrity. Our full service production company, publishing house, management, and media development firm promise to engage you creatively and honor you and ourselves, as well as the community, in order to bring about fulfillment and abundance both personally and professionally.

TVGuestpert & TVGuestpert Publishing are subsidiaries of Jacquie Jordan Inc.

BODY & SPIRIT / Inspiration & Personal Growth
Nationwide Distribution through Ingram & New Leaf

Book Cover by Jonathan Fong
Headshot Photography by Starla Fortunato
Book Design by Lynette Ubel – Ubel Design

Published by TVGuestpert Publishing
11664 National Blvd, #345
Los Angeles, CA. 90064
310-584-1504
www.TVGPublishing.com

First Printing February 2015
Printed in the United States of America
10 9 8 7 6 5 4 3 2 1

THE ART OF HAVING IT ALL:

A Woman's Guide to Unlimited Abundance

by *New York Times*
bestselling author
CHRISTY WHITMAN

DEDICATION:

*To my husband, Frederic Gobeil. Your love
and vision elevates me beyond what I can see
for myself. Thank you for all the ways you
show up in our relationship. You are my dream
and a huge part of my "it" and my "all."*

*To Alex and Maxim, thank you for
taking me on the craziest ride of my life.
The love that you give me, and the way you
receive me has expanded me beyond anything
I could have ever imagined. And to all of my
partners on the other side of the veil, thank
you for your guidance, and supporting
me when I ask for or need it.*

ACKNOWLEDGMENTS

During a conversation I had with Anna Trebunskya, she said, "Once your coach, always your coach." I couldn't agree more. The information that has enabled me to make the inner shifts necessary to create the life I am living today came to me through many extraordinary people, all of whom have had a profound impact on my life. My experiences with each of these individuals led me to greater awareness and clarity, and for this I am forever grateful:

To Frank Valesh, my father. Thank you for your work ethic and for your willingness to allow me to be me. I appreciate our relationship now more than ever. And I do know you are proud of me.

To Inez Valesh, my mother. I am grateful for our relationship and for how much more I enjoy being with you since I have done my inner healing. And I also know you are proud of me.

To Theresa Valesh, my sister. When you were in your body, you taught me so much of what not to do. Since you have transitioned, you have been one of my biggest partners on the other side.

To James Malinchak, Ti Caine, and Brendon Burchard. Through contrast I gained a lot of clarity from your coaching, helping, healing and consulting. You all have played a significant role in my development and growth, both personally and professionally.

To Melanie Flores, Rebecca Grado, Jennifer Bailey, David Morelli, Eva Gregory and especially Ken Stone, for being there for me when I really needed extra support in my life.

To Orin and DaBen, my first and most pivotal spiritual teachers, I am
so grateful for your influence in my life and my teachings. I am honored to
have the opportunity to pass on your wisdom and to empower more people
to live in light and love. I know you feel my gratitude and love.

To the non-physical teachers known as Abraham-Hicks. When I met
you, my entire life shifted completely, because it was you who first showed
me what a powerful creator I am. I am grateful for every interaction,
question that has been answered and all of the fun cruises we have shared
together.

To Karen Wilson, my mentor and spiritual teacher, you have saved
my life. I express more of my original nature because of your wisdom,
guidance, and the space you create for me to open up. Words can never
express the gratitude that I feel for you. Because of our relationship, I am
a better teacher and coach; wife and mother; daughter, friend, leader, and
human being.

To Adam Barta, Aimee Serafini, Aine Belton, Alexandra Allred,
Alexis Martin Neely, Allana Pratt, Amanda Righetti, Amethyst Wyldfyre,
Amy Ahlers, Andrea Albright, Andy Shaw, Ann Taylor, Anna Trebunskaya,
Asara Lovejoy, Ashley Turner, Arielle Ford, Baeth Davis, Bec Robbins,
Bill Harris, Brad Yates, Bob Proctor, Bob Doyle, Carol Look, Carol Tuttle,
Cathy Demers, Catherine Ewing, Chris Cade, Christa O'Leary, Christian
Mickelson, Christine Arylo, Christine Hassler, Christine Kloser, Claire
Zammit, Colete Baron-Reid, Cynthia Kersey, Cynthia Thaik, Dave Austin,
Dawn Clark, David Ricklan, Derek Rydall, Debra Poneman, Debbie
Allen, Debbie Millman, Dharma Rose, Dr. Eric Pearl, Eben Pagan, E.G. Daily,
Emmanuel Dagher, Eram Saeed, Erica Diamond, Erin Cox, Eva Gregory,
Fabienne Fredrickson, Dr. Fabrizio Mancini, Farhana Dhalla, Forbes Riley,

Gail Goodwin, GP Walsh, Heather Flemming, Heather Chauvin, Harrison Klein, Jack M. Zufelt, Jafree Ozwald, James Alvino, Jane Goldner, Janet Bray Attwood, Janet Clark, Jane Velez-Mitchell, Jay Fiset, Jeanna Gabellini, Jessica Ortner, Jennifer McClean, Jill Hope, Joan Sotkin, Judy O'Beirn, Jeff Gignac, Joe Nunziata, Jack Canfield, Dr. Joe Vitale, John Assaraf, John Burgos, Dr. John F. Demartini, John Gray, John Seeley, Karin Volo, Karen Lamark Wilson, Karl Moore, Kat Loterzo, Kelly Sullivan Walden, Keith Leon, Ken Foster, Ken Stone, Kristen Howe, Larry Ostrovsky, Laura Gisborne, Lillian Moore, Lily Jensen, Linda Joy, Lisa Bloom, Lisa Cherney, Lisa Coffey, Lisa Nichols, Lisa E. Zimmerman, Loral Langemeier, Dr. Rev. Louise-Diana, Marianne Williamson, Margaret Lynch, Marcia Wieder, Marci Shimoff, Mary Allen, Mary Morrissey, Maura Leon, Michael Losier, Mike Robbins, Michelle Gielan, Mindi Abair, Morgana Rae, Natalie Ledwell, Ocean Robbins, Pamela Bruner, Paul Hoffman, Paul R. Scheele, Ph.D., Peggy McColl, Ric Thompson, Rich German, Richard Luck, Rikka Zimmerman, Rob Burns, Roger Hamilton, Rolonda Watts, Ryan Harris, Sage Lavine, Dr. Sara Gottfried, Shanda Sumpter, Sheila Gale, Shelly Lefkoe, Sheri K. Hoff, Sonia Ricotti, Stacy Van Gogh, Steve Olsher, Sue Morter, Sunny Chayes, Dr. Symeon Rodger, Tabitha & Napoleon D'uomo, Tara Marino, Tellman Knudson, Trevor Justice, Tristan and Sabrina Truscott, Topher Morrison, and Twenty Twenty, all of whom I interviewed while researching this book. I appreciate each one of you for the amazing work you are doing to raise the consciousness of our planet and to support people in living happier, more abundant and more fulfilled lives. Thank you for the time, energy and wisdom you have contributed to forwarding the message that every one of us can have it all, as we want it and as we define it.

And to those that help me show up as a teacher, coach, and author by all that you do: To Danielle Dorman, without whose contribution this book literally would not have made it to print. I love to write, but you make what I write make sense. You are more than my editor. You are a dear friend, trusted confidant, and this baby's other mother.

To Jacquie Jordan, Stephanie Cobian, and the entire TVGuestpert team, it was because of our conversation that this book was birthed, and because of your expertise it has the potential of reaching so many women that need this message. Thank you for always holding the vision for me and my teaching. I know that is a gift that is beyond what words can express.

To My "Dream" Team, Terri Romine, Jonathan Hunsaker (my friend, brother, and business partner), Evelyn Apostolou (my dear friend, Maxim's Godmother, and reason I can do what I do), Tammy Lawman (the most amazing affiliate manager), Jenn Luna, Kelly Lewis, Julie Kleinhans, Rachel Christie, Fallon Pfifer, Kelly Catalano, and Theresa Hoermann (the most amazing assistant). I also want to thank all the mentors with the QSCA: George Carradini, Lola Love!, Sheila Callaham, Barbara Anselmi, Jenny Lee, Francine Landry, Deb Corey, Janet Bieschke, and Renee Marcou. You all help me as a World Server. You all do what I don't want to do and support me by laying the necessary groundwork. Thank you for all of your service and support. I love each of you. You are my family.

To Francine Remillard, it is because of your love and attention to Alexander and Maxim that I am able to give in service to the world. You are one in a million, and each day I am grateful for who you are and what you do. I am blessed to have you in my life.

— • —

TABLE OF CONTENTS

FOREWORD
by Anna Trebunskaya

No pain, no gain. As someone who's been a competitive dancer since
the age of seven, I'm pretty familiar with this philosophy – as I'm sure you
are as well. Some version of this mindset lies at the heart of most of the
strategies we're taught to help us succeed – not only in athletics, but in all
areas of life. We are told from a young age that hard work, striving to be
the best, and pushing ourselves to the limit is the path to realizing our
potential, fulfilling our heart's desires, and succeeding at everything we
want to accomplish. For over 25 years, my life was organized around this
principle, and with great discipline I followed a rigorous and predictable
schedule of training, traveling internationally, competing and performing.
What I've learned from experience is that while discipline and hard work are
essential to accomplishing goals, there is a limit to how much we can achieve
through these means alone. In fact, the blessings in my life that I cherish
the most – having the opportunity to perform in front of millions of televi-
sion viewers; teaching people how to move their bodies and feel good about
themselves; and most recently, becoming a mother to my precious daughter,
Amalya – were not necessarily planned, but came about as a result of simply
allowing myself to be moved in the direction that life seemed to be urging
me. Something I know now that I did not know ten years ago is that the
universe often holds a far bigger vision for us than we are capable of seeing
for ourselves at any particular moment in time. I've had to learn to embrace
change and understand that we need to move toward it in a fluid way, not
against it … it's very much like dancing.

My career as a competitive dancer has been tremendously rewarding, and yet over time, my drives and passions have changed. I now desire more from life than the high from jumping on four planes over the course of two days to perform in multiple shows. Constantly traveling from place to place, at times seeing only the inside of a studio, theater or ballroom and not enjoying the little things in life and on tour – the beautiful mountains in Colorado, Central Park in New York City, the ocean in Sarasota – made me realize that I was ready for a change and needed to take a step back. In my heart I sensed it, but I was so accustomed to living within the rigid structure of having every detail of my life planned out a solid year in advance, that even the idea of change made me uncomfortable. I was groomed to be a competitor – and truth be told, until recently, competing was the only thing I knew I could do and do well. But to continue traveling down that familiar path, I realized, would be to choose "routine" over opportunity and creativity. Life was urging me in a new, uncharted direction, and I could either keep fighting it, or I could go with the flow. Eventually, as the saying goes, I stopped trying to swim upstream against the proverbial river and instead allowed it to carry me. This approach of surrendering and allowing, versus forcing and controlling, has guided me to create a life that I love; a life in which I truly feel that I have it all.

The timing of meeting Christy and reading her work – particularly this book – could not have been more perfect, because Christy describes in language that is both universal and deeply practical, many of the same insights that I have come to know and recognize about my own life. Although I am only just beginning to learn about the laws of manifestation that Christy explains throughout these pages, I identified with all of them from my own personal experience. I was grateful for the addition of so many hands-on tools and real life examples she provides. I love that Christy has targeted women with her message, because in my experience, regardless of culture or race, women are hardwired toward perfectionism and control. This book brings home the point that doing it all is not the same as having it all. I can now say with certainty that having it all is not only about winning. It's a feeling we carry with us in the privacy of our own hearts and minds. For me, it's a combination of feeling thankful, hopeful, and healthy. *The Art of Having It All* will support you in charting a course not only to greater abundance and success, but to a deeper connection with yourself and an increased ability to enjoy all that you are and all that you have created and will create ... even if you don't have that plan yet!

— ● —

ANNA TREBUNSKAYA,
Professional Ballroom Dancer and TV Personality
Los Angeles, California

AUTHOR PREFACE

You and I are probably a lot alike. I'm in my early 40s. I'm married. I am the mother of two boys, ages four and five. I have a busy life, a household to run, and a full-time job (several of them, actually). I have lived through some difficult times – my sister's suicide, a divorce, and the open heart surgery of my newborn son, to name a few. I am also the founder of an internationally acclaimed coaching academy and the creator of a library of personal development programs that reach over 125,000 people each month. I am passionately in love with my husband, Frederic, who is also my business partner. I take time out every day to laugh with, talk with, and roll around on the floor with my kids. I work out regularly, get a massage every Saturday, take fantastic vacations, and have plenty of "me" time to dream, to go out with friends, or to kick back and just do nothing. Oh yeah, and I'm also making more money than I ever dreamed possible.

Just in case you're wondering; this was not always my reality. In fact, just seventeen years ago, I was unhappy in virtually every aspect of my life. I was thirty pounds overweight and nearly $60,000 in debt. I worked at a job I hated, and had a knack for attracting the "wrong" kind of men. I tried everything I could think of to change the circumstances of my life, believing that affecting outer change was the key to inner happiness. Nothing worked, and as a result, my life felt like a constant, uphill struggle.

So, how did I get from where I was then to where I am today? The answer is simple: I learned about the universal laws that govern deliberate creation, I applied them in my life, and almost immediately, my reality began to transform. As I write these words, I can honestly say that I have manifested everything I have ever wanted and have created a life in which I truly *have it all* – spontaneously and effortlessly. This book is a culmination of my conviction that every woman can have it all, as she defines it, in this and in each evolving moment in her life. This message may challenge your notions of what you believe to be possible for you and your life; unfortunately, the misconception that having it all is impossible and even detrimental to our well-being has gained a real foothold in the minds of many American women. A recent case in point:

I was invited to a media summit in New York where I met with dozens of TV and radio producers all looking for experts in various fields to write feature articles for their magazines or appear as guests on their shows. One woman I met was a freelance writer for *New York* magazine. Confident that I had the perfect angle for her magazine's demographic, I approached her and asked, "Do you know what all New York women want?" "No. What?" she replied. "They want it all," I said, handing her my media one sheet and contact information. Her reaction was intense and immediate. "Women can't have it all!" she snapped – and then began telling me about a newly released book written by a prominent business woman who justifies exactly why this is so. According to this author, she explained, what we women need to do is lower our expectations, not raise them, and that to seek fulfillment in all areas of life simultaneously is unrealistic, at best. At worst, she said, it's a sure recipe for overwhelm and stress. Then she asked me point blank: "Do you know any woman who truly has it all?" "Yes," I replied. "I know many, and I am one of them." I then proceeded to share with her some of the facts about my life I have created: "I have created a business that I love, coaching people to create abundance and success in all aspects of their lives. I have a happy marriage and two healthy, hilarious, and conscious children. I am physically healthy and in great shape. I run a multi-million dollar business from the comfort of a beautiful and spacious home, and work when I want to and because I want to, not because I have to. I have time for myself and my family, I laugh a lot, I am blessed with a powerful spiritual connection that is a continual source of inspiration. I have a great support system…" She cut me off mid-sentence and handed me back the paper I had given her. "I won't be needing this," she said, "because I don't believe that any woman can have it all." I looked her in the eyes as I took the piece of paper back and said, "Therein lies the problem." And then I walked away.

To say that I was exasperated by this encounter would be a huge understatement. Here was a writer for a national magazine, in a position to send a powerful message to a wide readership of success-minded professionals, who was not only arguing for her own limitations but making a blanket statement which affirmed the limitations of *all* women. Clearly, I thought, there must exist some misinformation or misinterpretation in the minds of women about what *having it all* really means. Contrary to popular belief, having it all is not about striving for perfection, or about living our lives according to someone else's standards or expectations. It's not about working ourselves to a state of exhaustion, spreading ourselves too thin, or trading inner peace and contentment for outer trinkets of success. The intention of this book is to upend these misconceptions, and to show women – *all women* – that not only is it possible to have it all, but to settle for anything less is to deprive ourselves of the exhilaration, joy, expansion and freedom of becoming all that we are capable of being. We were meant to have it all; to continually give birth to new desires and to fulfill them. It is the nature of the universe to expand – and we are part of the universe and all-that-is. Our ability to expand, to achieve, and to evolve is truly limitless.

All we need to do is look to the natural world around us to realize that the universe we live in is one of unlimited energy and unlimited abundance: There are over 200 billion stars in the Milky Way galaxy, which is just one in hundreds of millions of galaxies. There is enough water combined in the world's oceans that if you poured it over the United States, it would cover the entire land ninety miles deep. In the next sixty seconds alone, the sun will generate enough solar power to fulfill the energy needs of our entire planet for a year. Because we were born into this abundant universe, there is virtually no limit to how much love, inspiration, joy, excitement, success or abundance we can experience. The concept of lack is entirely man-made; nowhere in nature do we find evidence of it. Abundance is our original state of being.

So the question arises: When there is evidence of abundance all around us, why are so many people living lives of lack and discontent? Why are women in particular arguing for their limitations rather than embracing their dreams and getting busy learning how to manifest them? The answer is that most of us have been so steeped in a mindset of lack and scarcity that the true abundance we are seeking – of love, of vitality, of well-being, success and happiness – simply isn't available to us. Having it all demands that we step out of this mindset and acknowledge that because abundance is our very nature, we have the ability to manifest our *it* and *all*, independent of whether other women are choosing this for themselves or not. Yes, this is "another" book about deliberate creation, but one that has teeth. I stand by every one of the principles you will learn here, not because they sound good in theory, but because I have used them to create turnaround after turnaround in virtually every aspect of my life. This book is the culmination of all that I have learned, applied, and successfully taught others for over ten years. I don't practice what I preach; I preach what I have practiced – because it works.

What I can promise you – both from my own experience and from my experience in coaching thousands of other women – is this: Whatever your circumstances, it is never too late to re-create yourself and your life to reflect your evolving definition of what it means to have it all. Where you have been is inconsequential. All that matters is that you know where you are now and where you desire to be. There is a gap between what you want and what you currently have. In this book, I will teach you how to understand, practice, and utilize the Universal Laws of Sufficiency and Abundance, Detachment, Attraction, Allowing, Polarity, and Pure Potentiality to effortlessly and joyfully bridge that gap in virtually every aspect of your life.

Let's get this party started!

—— ● ——

CHRISTY WHITMAN
Montreal, Canada

"There is no one right path.
There are endless paths,
and the differences
in the paths are what make
them more and more,
and more, perfect."

– ABRAHAM-HICKS

CHAPTER **1:**
Defining Your *It* and Your *All*

Discovering our *it* and our *all* is a deeply personal mission that each one of us undertakes for ourselves. No two women have the same life experiences, the same perspectives, the same goals, preferences, beliefs or ideals... and for this reason, no two women define having it all in exactly the same ways. Each and every one of us is a unique expression of the Divine, and – despite what we may have been socialized to believe – we don't all want the same things. I know many women who thrive on devoting the lion's share of their time and attention to their careers. For them, work is a primary source of empowerment and self-esteem, and the fulfillment they derive from this area spills over into all others. Some women are wired the exact opposite, and having it all for them is centered around building a happy marriage and family life. I know women for whom friendships with other girlfriends are a major source of fulfillment, and others who get those social needs met through work, political activism, and other outlets. There are a growing number of women who are consciously deciding not to have children and to channel their energy instead into building a different type of community, or into a life of philanthropy and service. As a matter of fact, the cover of a 2013 issue of *Time* magazine featured the headline, "When Having It All Means Not Having Kids." My friend Dawn, whom I've known since seventh grade, is a perfect example. As long as I've known her, Dawn has been completely clear that marriage and children were not part of her equation for having it all. Acknowledging that her decision was conscious and made totally by her own design, she then successfully attracted a partner who shares her values. Although they have never been married, Brannon and Dawn have been creating a beautiful and happy life together for over twenty-one years. Having it all is having everything we desire in each aspect of our self-expression, and in the proportion that is perfect for each one of us. One woman's idea of "balance" will be another woman's nightmare.

Because each one of us comes into this world with a unique set of circumstances, challenges, opportunities and desires, there are literally as many different definitions of having it all as there are women (and men) on the planet. Even for the same woman, our ideas about what we want out of life change and evolve as we do – from year to year, day to day, and from moment to moment. When I was single, a central component to creating my *it* and *all* was finding my ideal partner. Once I magnetized him into my life (I'll tell you *that* story a little later), I next wanted to create a home with him. After we got married and moved into our ideal house, we wanted a child – and on and on it goes. We never get it all done, because the moment we create something new, that new vantage point brings our awareness to a new desire to create something different or more. Life is a process of defining and redefining what we want, and as a result, our desires are continually under revision. There is no final destination. Once we reach the top, the "mountain" we are now in the process of climbing becomes nothing more than a vista from which we can see the next mountain we want to climb.

Sometimes, when I first introduce a woman to the possibility that she can have it all, the idea is met with some internal resistance that goes something like this: "Having it all is not possible, because it's not possible for me to own EVERY pair of shoes ever made. I can't personally take EVERY amazing vacation there is to take or go on EVERY possible adventure. I can't own EVERY house or car or boat, or have ALL the money there is in the world." And, of course, this is absolutely correct. At the most simplistic and materialistic level, we can't have all the money in the world or own all the beautiful shoes that were ever created in the same way we can't do everything that is possible to do all at once. We can't learn to be a pilot at the same time we're learning to ballroom dance or become a sushi chef, because we do have one limitation in life and that limitation is time. But here's the thing: While it's true that there are limitations as to how much we can have or experience at any given time, and while it may not be possible for any one person to own all the material possessions in the world, the real question is – who would want to?

I remember a couple of years ago I was having a conversation with my friend's son, Mark, who was about eight years old at the time. I told him that because there is no end to the universe we live in, there is no end to the possibilities that we can create for ourselves or our lives. He thought about this for a minute and then said, "Not everything is possible," so I asked him to tell me something that he wanted that would be impossible for him to create. I think he was just waiting for the chance to challenge my theory because he instantly fired back, "It's not possible for me to fit a spaceship inside my nose." That visual gave us both a good laugh, but the point is, Mark didn't have a genuine desire to fit a spaceship inside his nose. After chatting a bit more, I learned that what Mark *did* have was a genuine desire to experience outer space and that, specifically, he wanted to feel what it was like to be floating and weightless. Now, is being in space and having the sensation of floating and weightlessness an experience that is possible for Mark to create for himself? Absolutely! Having our *it* and *all* is not about doing or having or being every possible thing there is to do and have and be. It's about manifesting those experiences in life that call our attention and that speak to our unique values, dreams, hopes and desires. It's as though each of us is looking at life through a kaleidoscope. What we see when we envision the kind of life we want to create is a function of the particular combination of filters we are viewing it through.

Another important thing to distinguish is that the way we define our *it* and *all* varies not only from woman to woman and from decade to decade, but also exists on two different levels simultaneously: First, there is the materialistic dimension of how we want our lives to look on a purely physical level – the condition of our bodies, our homes, our relationships, our finances, careers, etc. And second, there is the non-physical dimension of having it all, which is the internal feeling experience we have about ourselves and our lives. Both dimensions are important, and as you'll learn, the inner experience of having it all is what allows us to attract, receive and enjoy the outer manifestation.

Having it all in a material sense is simply a matter of identifying the aspects of life that we value the most and then deciding how we want those aspects to be. For example, I have it all in a physical sense when my body is healthy and toned, full of energy and at the proper size to fit into my clothes. I have it all when my husband Frederic and I are relating in a way that is intimate and vulnerable – when we are bringing out the very best in one another, laughing a lot, and enjoying the journey of being co-creators as spiritual companions, lovers, parents, and friends. I have it all when my communication with my kids is fun and flowing – when I am patient and present and have the experience of being deeply connected to them and them to me. I have it all when I feel the complete support of all the amazing people who work with me (I call them my Dream Team) when an idea will be born within me, and then the perfect person will come along who takes joy in helping me bring it to fruition. I have it all when I can be with my parents, free from any tinges of resentment or from wanting to change them, and I am able to simply enjoy them and the time I have left with them. I have it all when I'm attending the annual charity event for the hospital that saved my son's life (more on that later, too), and when I am in a position to give generously to such a worthwhile organization.

Sometimes the experience of having it all bubbles up in me when I recognize the simple ways in which I am truly blessed, like last month when I was hanging out in one of my favorite cities (Chicago), with my dearest friend (Dawn), having lunch with my boys at one of my favorite restaurants (Penny's Noodles) and ordering a Cosmo to celebrate. Other times the feeling manifests in response to a day that seems perfectly balanced: I manage to get in a great workout, spend quality time with both my boys and with Frederic, and contribute to my business in a way that leaves me inspired and fulfilled. And, because my work is about teaching abundance, for me another important aspect of having it all is creating wealth in a material sense: being free of debt, having enough money in the bank to be able to purchase what I want when I want, to invest a large amount of money each year to grow my wealth, and to give freely to those I love. In the area of my self-expression and career, I have it all when I know that my creativity, talents and passion are being channeled productively and in a way that makes a difference in the lives of those who are drawn to my work.

When these external conditions are present in my tangible, physical experience, I experience a sense of personal fulfillment because these conditions remind me that I have the power to deliberately create my outer reality to align with any inner desire. And yet – and this is a big "yet" – the external conditions themselves are *not* the source of my fulfillment. In fact, it's actually the other way around: the fulfillment that comes from knowing that I am a whole, complete and abundant being is what draws into my life the external circumstances that match and mirror back to me my inner feeling of fulfillment. All tangible, external manifestations are first created in the unseen, internal dimension of our inner experience. *Having it all* simply means having access to all of yourself, in any moment you choose it, and in every aspect of life that is important to you.

> "Having it all *simply means having access to all of yourself, in any moment you choose it, and in every aspect of life that is important to you.*"

The experience of having it all, for me, is knowing in every cell of my being that I already am everything that I seek. My very nature is abundance, love, connection, joy. When I am aligned with and vibrating in alignment with this truth, I am full of myself in the very purest sense – not full of ego, but full of my original nature and allowing the highest expression of myself to come forth. I am able to feel and embrace the whole range of my human emotions; one shifting into the other, without avoidance or resistance. I am not attached to other people's opinions, or to trying to gain their approval. My "feel good" is not dependent on the way anyone else behaves, because I know that I am free to choose how I want to feel in any given moment.

The inner experience of having it all is one of being fully connected to the life force that is the source of all manifested things and to know and feel that we are an integral part of that source and of all-that-is. It is being here and present; awake and alive; not blocking or cutting off any part of ourselves, but allowing all aspects of who we are to be seen and to shine. This is the true joy in living, because without this inner connection to self, our outer accomplishments are shallow and fleeting. They entertain us momentarily but don't really nourish our souls. This explains why, in the world of outer appearances, we can have all the "things" we think will make us happy and still feel empty, restless, unfulfilled or discontent inside.

The Jig Is Up

By "jig," I mean the act of looking for happiness outside of ourselves (or in the words of that song from the 70s, "looking for love in all the wrong places"). I'm here to tell you that this jig is up. In the same way that the appearance of happiness does not automatically translate into actual happiness, the outer manifestation of our *it* and *all* does not automatically generate the internal contentment, satisfaction, peace of mind or happiness that we are taught we will feel in the having of it. The late, great, comedian George Carlin expressed this point in his unique and brilliant way: "Trying to be happy by accumulating possessions is like trying to satisfy hunger by taping sandwiches all over your body." Inner satiation doesn't necessarily come about as a result of external wealth. If you doubt this, take a stroll through a ballroom of an exclusive country club or the living room of the family down the street who sends out the Normal Rockwell Christmas card every year and whose lawn is always perfectly manicured. Or visit an ashram in India or a simple farm in a remote part of the world. What you'll see is that people who appear to have it all in an outer, material sense may or may not have it all in an internal, spiritual sense – and vice versa.

"Trying to be happy by accumulating possessions is like trying to satisfy hunger by taping sandwiches all over your body."

Most of us grew up in a culture where, from the time we're young, we've been conditioned to work on ourselves until we create the "perfect" picture of what we think our lives "should" look like, because once we get the picture perfect, we will be happy. When our inner reality doesn't match the outer pictures we've created, we naturally feel disillusioned or even devastated. The experience is one of, *so I "have it all." Now what??* In the absence of the inner experience of having it all, the external manifestation of it has little meaning and can actually bring more stress and anxiety than happiness or comfort.

Twelve years ago I was living inside the perfect picture of what I believed my life was supposed to look like: I had the good-looking husband and the big beautiful dream home, complete with two cute little dogs. I drove a nice car and had a successful and financially rewarding career. We had friends and neighbors who were close to us in age and who shared (at the time) similar goals. We went to dinner parties on Saturday nights and had back-yard barbecues on Sundays. On the outside, it truly was a perfect picture. I had succeeded in filling my life with all the "stuff" that I had been taught – from my parents, from peers, from our culture and even from fairy tales – would make me happy. I had it all in an external sense. The problem was that the having of it didn't change the way I felt inside; there was just more stuff around me. Even worse is that after creating the husband, the house, the car, the body, and the career, I was actually *unhappier,* because now the jig was up. If happiness was not the natural byproduct of having it all in an external sense, then where does it come from? What is its true source?

I realized that everything I had created on the outside was an attempt to compensate for feeling inadequate on the inside. Even in the presence of all the "things" I had created, something was missing, because I was cut off from myself and the true source of my light. I was still operating from early conditioning and programming that told me that who I am is not good enough. Marrying the "perfect" person and buying the "perfect" house were in my mind outcomes that would finally prove that I was good enough. Everything I created externally was for the purpose of making me happy inside, and like a good drug, it did the trick – for a while. There was a certain thrill of being engaged in the pursuit of the next accomplishment and the next one after that. But after I had succeeded in creating all the things that I'd been programmed to believe would make me happy, I still didn't feel happy. I was disconnected to the larger part of myself. I did not feel my power. I did not appreciate the moment, and I did not know I could actually choose to feel better. My soul was searching for deeper meaning and a sense of being more authentically connected to myself, but nothing I created externally provided these things. In fact, the more I had, the emptier I felt.

When we find ourselves living in a situation that looks good from the outside but no longer brings us inner joy, we can choose one of two paths: we can deny or repress our discontent and "shrink" ourselves so we continue to fit into a life that is too small or no longer serves us; or we can embrace the new direction our soul is urging us toward, and make the choice not to shrink, but to stretch. The first path leads to depression, resignation and chronic discontent. The second path brings exhilaration, freedom, and an ever-deepening experience of fulfillment. What most people label as depression is really a *suppression* of our innate desire to expand into the magnificent women we were born to be. Author and spiritual teacher, GP Walsh – whom I interviewed for this book – describes depression as a cultural conditioning in which we are taught to "lower our expectations rather than open our perspective." To have it all is to continually come up against our evolutionary edge – where we have gone as far as we can go with one particular form of our self-expression and are being asked to let that go and move to the next. As our priorities change, so do our desires, and this means that sometimes we outgrow circumstances that we once found to be completely fulfilling.

The need to recognize and honor shifting priorities was underscored by my friend and colleague, Arielle Ford, a beautiful and brilliant woman and the author of *The Soulmate Secret*, when I asked her recently how she defines *having it all* for herself. "I finally figured out how to prioritize," she said. "For years, I lived in this constant state of ambition and overwork and overwhelm. The way I live my life today is what I refer to as 'unbranded.' Because while I *could* be running all over the country lecturing or leading workshops, that choice would not support my definition of what having it all means to me at this moment in my life. Why would I want to be in a ballroom in St. Louis or Kansas City when my soulmate is sitting in our dream home in California?" Having it all does not mean doing it all, and the great news is, we get to pick and choose what we give our attention to, and – if one choice no longer fulfills one of our *it* and *all* desires, we can choose something else.

"The way I live my life today is what I refer to as 'unbranded.'"

There is no stopping the evolution of our desire, because desire is the driving force behind all creation. Life was never meant to stand still. We were never meant to say "This is it – I now have everything I will ever want!" – in the same way we would never want a waiter to bring us all the food we will ever want to eat in a lifetime in one serving. To be alive is to be continually hungry and then full; to be restless and discontented; to want more, to create more – and to become more as a result of all of it.

There will never be another you. There will never be anyone exactly like you, with your experiences, your perspective, your thoughts and ideas… and no one but you has the exact same true heartfelt desires. These desires are not meant to be suppressed or ignored. We were meant to fulfill them – without exception or limitation. It is the birthright of every woman to make manifest our *it* and our *all* – whatever that means to us at each changing moment of our lives. Whatever it is you desire, that desire would not have been born within you if you didn't also have the potential to fulfill it. The very fact that you can think about and feel the presence of this new desire means that it's possible for you to create it in this abundant universe. Even though in our minds we can't see the possibility, if there is a desire, there is also a way. As Napoleon Hill noted back in the 20th century, "Whatever the mind can conceive and believe, it can achieve."

"Whatever the mind can conceive and believe, it can achieve."

— • —

PLAY SHEET FOR CHAPTER 1:
Defining Your *It* and Your *All*

Give yourself permission to envision what *having it all* means to you in each important area of your life. Let your imagination expand to create a vision of all that you desire to create – physically, emotionally, socially, financially, and spiritually. Visualize a reality in which your desires manifest naturally and easily, and in which you experience all the joy, health, success, abundance and fulfillment that you desire. What are the things that truly bring you happiness? What conditions or experiences have you always wanted to create? If you could design your life to be amazing beyond your wildest imagination, what would it look like? How would it feel? Are you financially abundant and debt free? Is your body a certain size or weight? Do you feel more rewarded in your career? Are your relationships more intimate and satisfying? To the best of your ability, allow yourself to receive any thoughts and ideas about what having it all means to you and acknowledge them without censoring yourself or worrying about how they are going to manifest.

Visit www.TheArtOfHavingItAll.com to do an experiential, guided process that will support you in creating a clear image of what having it all means to you.

CHAPTER **2:**
The Handbook to Ultimate Disempowerment
(aka Why You Don't Yet Have It All)

Now that you've defined what *it* and *all* looks like for you, the logical question to ask is, why don't you already have it? Well, for starters, it's because like a good girl – and whether you are aware of this or not – you have been following the rules of an unwritten rulebook handed down to you by your parents, teachers, friends, bosses and everyone else whose love and acceptance you craved. Let me explain:

When we are born, we are wide open, unbounded, and virtually unlimited in the number of possibilities we can create. Life stretches out in front of us like an empty chalkboard – a blank slate. Our self-expression is uncalculated and we are one hundred percent ourselves. Modifying our behavior to be more "pleasing" to others is a foreign concept, and love is a given – not something that we have to earn. For most of us, early childhood is a time of joy, adventure, grace and wonder. Then at some point in our young lives – as a result of experiences we have with our parents, siblings, peers, teachers, or sometimes even complete strangers – we learn that there are conditions to what we once perceived as an unconditional existence, and we learn that to secure love and acceptance, we must comply with them.

So, what are the rules of this unwritten handbook, you ask?
Here are a few:

It's selfish to listen to yourself and do what makes you happy, so do what others think you should do and make them happy instead. Be constantly on the lookout for what others think about you, because what they think of you is WAY more important than what you think of yourself. There is only so much love, attention, and success to go around – so you better fight for your share – but don't become too successful or shine too brightly because then others will reject you. Who are you to be THAT successful, anyway? You are not enough as you are, so you better work hard to gain the love and acceptance of others…

Scripts like these are being played out behind the scenes of our conscious awareness – as the internal conversations we continually have with ourselves; as the moods, attitudes and emotions we offer in response to people and situations; and in the thoughts we think and the choices we make. They are the result of early conditioning that we receive from our parents and caregivers – usually well intentioned – which lead us to the false conclusion that who we are naturally is somehow inadequate or inappropriate. Dr. Symeon Rodger, known as the "Warrior Coach," whom I interviewed while writing this book, described our early childhood conditioning beautifully, explaining that we are taught to "Put away everything we are interested in and start fitting in. The message we receive is one of 'sacrifice yourself – your interests and who you are at your essence – for the sake of your family, your culture, your fill-in-the-blank.' We are literally taught to lose touch with who we are, and then once we're in our 30s, 40s and 50s and someone asks us, 'What do you want your life to look like and feel like?', we don't have a clue, because we haven't thought about it since we were in our late teens and thought about it all the time." This early conditioning directly informs the life scripts that tell us who we are, what we are capable of, and what parts of ourselves are and are not okay to express. But how exactly are these internal scripts created, and how do they come to have such a great influence on the way we relate to life?

As children who are literally dependent on the love and support of others, we strive from an early age to make our caregivers happy. The first fallacy, of course, is that we have the power to make others happy, but it's easy to understand how we come to believe this: When we do something that our parents or caregivers approve of, we are rewarded with a big smile or a hug. When, on the other hand, we do something that makes Mommy or Daddy unhappy, we do not receive their positive attention. We then begin to modify our behavior in order to keep receiving the love and approval we need. In shifting our focus from making ourselves happy to striving to make others happy, we create a separation in our connection with ourselves. The attention we once placed on ourselves and on feeling good is now redirected to those who are in the position to care for us and to making sure *they* feel good. Those of us in particular who grew up in a chaotic environment, in which our bond to one or both parents was unstable or insecure, learn early on to become hyper-sensitive to even the slightest shift in the emotional tone of the household. At the young age of two or three, many of us were already accomplished people-pleasers.

Maybe we took on the role of keeping the peace in the family by being the good girl, or easing the adults' burdens by becoming the responsible girl, or the one that doesn't cause any problems or make any waves. Whatever early strategies we employed to keep our caregivers happy, and therefore attentive to our needs, inevitably fail for the simple reason that we don't have the power to make anyone happy besides ourselves. In the moment, however, we view our "failure" to please as a character flaw within us – "If Mommy and Daddy aren't showing me love, it must be because I am unlovable." From these core-wounding experiences, we form conclusions that shape and mold our identities, determining what we believe to be true about ourselves and how much or how little love, fulfillment and ease we believe we deserve. What was once a blank slate slowly gets filled in with conditions, restrictions and limitations. Instead of looking at life through the lens that anything is possible, we now see, hear, sense and let in only those possibilities that we already believe are possible. Suddenly, instead of having the experience that life is wide open and limitless, we have the experience that life is limited. And tragically, instead of feeling and behaving like the powerful creators we are, we begin to adopt the role of being a victim.

The scared 3-year-old who decides that she isn't lovable; the rejected 13-year-old who decides that she doesn't belong; the overwhelmed 19-year-old who decides that life is a struggle which must be conquered alone are each acting out a script written long ago that dictates what is and is not possible for herself and her life. Beliefs such as "I'm not confident," "I don't fit in," "Nobody understands me," or "It's not safe to express how I feel" are all examples of decisions made as a result of some core-wounding experience. These decisions often occur so early on in our lives that they become part of our thinking process without our conscious permission – and yet they shape the way we define ourselves and therefore direct the course of our lives. Said another way, we form an identity that is founded on our experience of not being enough, of being less than or undeserving, and then relate to that identity as if it's the truth. If left unchecked, these decisions – made long ago in the past and from the limited perspective of a child – become our present beliefs and the operating system we use to create our future. Everything we perceive, interpret, create and experience as our reality is filtered through what we believe is and is not possible.

Beliefs ➤ Thoughts ➤ Feelings ➤ Actions ➤ Outcomes

Our beliefs inform our thoughts, which then influence the way we feel, direct the actions we take and don't take, and – ultimately – determine the results we manifest in our lives. When almost a hundred years ago Henry Ford asserted that "Whether you think you can or think you can't, you're right," he was pointing to the ways in which our beliefs color our perception of "reality" by filtering the millions of possible outcomes that could come into being and drawing our attention only to those which we already think we can attain.

When our beliefs are in alignment with our desires – meaning that we are certain both about what we want and about our ability to attain it – we view every person, circumstance and opportunity as an ally. But if we are guided by an internal script that tells us that focusing on our own happiness is selfish; that becoming too successful will cause us to lose love; or that we need to be perfect in order to earn other people's approval or acceptance, we lock ourselves into a mindset of lack and limitation which drastically limits the amount of abundance we are open and available to receive – and this of course serves only to reinforce our limiting beliefs. I am neither a scientist nor a biochemist, but it's essential to understand that our beliefs don't just affect our thinking process; they trigger a powerful alchemical reaction throughout our physical bodies as well.

The Science of Belief

Our mind/body network is made up of trillions of cells, and every cell contains millions of receptor sites that allow us to receive, interpret and respond to the energy and information that comes to us from the environment. At birth, these receptor sites are open and permeable, but as we grow and form beliefs about ourselves and life, each receptor site gets imprinted with a particular blueprint that tells us how to perceive, interpret and react in any given situation. Beliefs rooted in lack and limitation get implanted in our sponge-like little minds long before we understand that we have the power to question them – and once they are imprinted on these receptor sites, they operate at a cellular level far beneath the level of our conscious awareness. Until we learn that we are at choice in the matter, this biological and emotional reaction happens automatically, in the same way our bodies respond to a threatening situation by releasing adrenaline to prepare us for fight or flight. This occurs, of course, whether the "threat" is real or imagined.

Let's break this process down into more familiar terms. If a woman desires to be in an intimate relationship but believes that there is a scarcity of "good" single men, the imprint of that belief will actually block her receptor sites from receiving any new or contradictory information. What she will find instead is evidence that supports the belief she already holds to be true: she meets someone she likes, but he turns out to be married, gay, or otherwise uninterested or unavailable. The moment her old belief is triggered, a biological reaction occurs in the very cells of her body which causes her to experience at a very concrete and physical level that her belief is valid and true. This is what is called a self-fulfilling prophecy: The more evidence she finds to support her belief, the more deeply that belief gets imprinted within her.

Beliefs are simply thoughts that have been thought over and over again. Like a well-worn path that leads from Point A to Point B, they create specific neuropathways within our mind/body circuitry. Of course these pathways are extremely helpful in the sense that they enable us to not have to re-think everything we see or do in our lives – we don't have to continually relearn, for example, the idea that "This is a chair," or that "This is blue." Once we have come to know and believe something as true, we can take a shortcut instead. But our beliefs cease to be helpful when in the same way our brains take a shortcut each time we see a chair or the color blue, we also assume something to be true in the present that we concluded to be true in the past.

Every belief that we hold to be true gives rise to a certain frequency of thoughts – and every thought triggers a range of emotions. Like everything in the universe, beliefs are made up of energy. Beliefs that are aligned with the energy of limitlessness and possibility magnetize greater possibilities into our lives. Beliefs that are contrary to our nature – what some people call "negative" beliefs – limit the range of what we allow ourselves to experience and hold us apart from the very things we desire. Our outdated, limiting beliefs exist not as just some mental construct, but as a real, palpable energy that permeates both body and mind. To release a belief that no longer serves, we need to be willing to feel this energy and take an honest look at how it is manifesting in our lives. We always create what we believe to be true, so we will always find "proof" that reality operates the way we think it does.

I remember hearing long ago, and before I ever became a mom, that once a family has a child, everyone gets sick because the child brings germs from daycare or preschool back into the home. When I became pregnant years later, people around me reinforced this idea, telling us that we'd better "Watch out, because once your baby is born, you are going to constantly get sick." Because the ground had already been laid, this suggestion went into my consciousness like a seed being planted in fertile soil – despite the fact that I was an adult who already understood the power of our thoughts and beliefs. Sure enough, after our boys were born, they did spend time at the daycare of the gym where I worked out, and they did get sick frequently.

Then I started getting sick – a lot. For almost a year I was down with a cold at least once a month, until I finally got sick of being sick and began examining my beliefs around the subject. I then realized that I had been giving my power away to a source outside of myself and allowing the beliefs of others who had experienced this before me to influence my perception of reality. As soon as I became aware of this belief and deliberately took responsibility for my own immune system, I went from being sick once a month to not having a cold in well over a year. The good news about beliefs is that they are a sword which cuts both ways: if you change what you believe, you change what you experience.

If you are unaware of your core beliefs in some key area of your life, it's easy enough to discover them. All you need to do is reflect on the current condition of that area of your life and ask yourself, "What would I need to believe – about myself, other people, or the world – in order to create this particular circumstance?" I asked myself this question years ago, when I was in the habit of spending more than I earned, and made the ends meet each month by going deeper and deeper into credit card debt. My belief at the time was that the company I worked for was the sole source of my income. I have to laugh now when I think about that, but when I honestly looked at what belief would have me stay in a job I didn't love even though I never had enough money at the end of the month to pay my bills, I had to admit to the limitations of my thinking when it came to my financial abundance. I had become so attached to receiving a paycheck every two weeks that I couldn't conceive of any other way of making money.

The day I changed this belief and accepted that my abundance comes from Source – not from any person or circumstance – I began to see the company I worked for as one of a limitless number of avenues through which money could come into my life. The more I embodied this belief, the more evidence I found to support it. Money began to stream in from a wide variety of sources. A year or so later, after redefining that abundance to me was less about making money and more about making a profit, I adopted an even more powerful belief: "I create *profits* like nobody's business." It became my daily mantra, and that is exactly what started to happen. Within months I was debt free, and after two years of working full time in my coaching business, I was finally making a profit (and a healthy one).

What's important to understand is that your outdated or limiting beliefs are not "wrong." Chances are, you adopted them because there was a time in your life when they served you, protected you, or kept you from feeling pain. Maybe there was a time when love really couldn't be trusted, or maybe you actually have had the experience that success always comes at a price. But to the extent that we allow these ancient beliefs to dictate our present moment choices, we continue to give them the power to direct the course of what unfolds in our future.

Our beliefs are self-fulfilling, and they are potent. They explain why when we see someone enjoying a degree of abundance, joy, success and happiness that we don't believe is possible for us, we deflect it. We might get jealous or explain it away as luck. Maybe we feel sorry for ourselves because we haven't yet created what they have, or invent stories about what they must be sacrificing to make ourselves feel better. These are all ways that we justify our current reality and ensure that we continue to create more of the same. Unless we – at the deepest level and in the privacy of our own innermost thoughts and feelings – believe that we are capable and deserving of enjoying that same degree of abundance, we won't allow ourselves to even entertain it as a possibility.

Our beliefs are only "true" if we empower them to be. At every moment we can choose a belief that pulls us towards our greatness rather than towards our limitations. As you'll learn in the chapters that follow, it's the energetic frequency that we send out through our thoughts, feelings, perceptions and beliefs that either repels or attracts our desires. Having it all is a process of attraction that happens from the inside out.

— ● —

PLAY SHEET FOR CHAPTER 2:
The Handbook to Ultimate Disempowerment (aka Why You Don't Yet Have It All)

Connecting with your vision of having it all in each key area of your life, ask yourself, "Do I believe it is possible for me to create this?" Listen to the answer as it comes to you, and allow yourself to identify the core beliefs that holds you apart from creating what you desire. Where are your beliefs aligned with scarcity or unworthiness rather than possibility and abundance?

Contemplating each of these limiting beliefs, see if you can identify where they came from. Notice how old you were when you adopted this worldview, and whether it still serves the woman you are today, or if you have outgrown it. In what areas of your life does this belief limit you?

As you consider the ways this belief manifests in your life, allow yourself to connect to the very energy of it. Does it have a particular form or color? Where and how does it exist in your body and mind? Breathe into this energy and as you do, imagine that it is being released, and the space that it once occupied is now empty and receptive. Remember that every time you untangle and release a limiting belief, you expand your energy field to allow in more of what you really want.

Bring to mind again your vision of a life in which you have it all, and as you breathe into the new space liberated by the release of your old belief, ask yourself what new belief would best support you in manifesting this vision. Is it a belief that the universe has enough for everyone? That there is enough to go around? That you deserve to have all that you desire? Whatever that new belief is, breathe it in.

CHAPTER **3:**
Creation From the Inside Out

The understanding that our beliefs filter the way we experience "reality" gives us an important clue to the hidden mechanism that governs creation: Everything we experience in the external, manifested world is a direct reflection of what we are experiencing within the internal world of our perception. Life is a dance between inner and outer; between the spiritual and the material; between energy and matter. This is because as human beings, we exist on multiple dimensions simultaneously. There is the part of us that is tangible and manifested – the part that exists in physical form; that interacts with other forms; that takes physical, concrete action. Underlying the physical aspect of us is our non-physical essence – the inner realm where our thoughts, beliefs, perceptions, desires and emotions are formed – that is always present, whether we are at rest or in motion and whether we are awake or asleep. The broader, non-physical aspect of us breathes life into the physical, and the physical aspect of us is a visible out-picturing of the part of us that is non-physical. Both realms of our existence are inseparable, in the same way that the front of your hand is inseparable from the back of your hand.

We now know, both from physics and modern science as well as from timeless wisdom, that energy – not matter – is the basis of everything that exists in the universe. Even things that appear to our senses as solid matter – rocks, mountains, trees, that spare tire that sometimes mysteriously appears across your midsection – are made up entirely of energy. In fact, it's been said that only 4 percent of our being manifests as material form, while 96 percent of us exists as pure, unmanifested, energetic potential – formless, malleable, and intangible. In the words of the 20th century French philosopher Pierre Teilhard de Chardin, "We are not human beings who have occasional spiritual experiences; we are spiritual beings having an occasional human experience." We may identify ourselves with our bodies, but our bodies represent only the tip of the metaphoric iceberg of the whole beings that we truly are. We are pure, unbounded consciousness that is temporarily focused right here, right now, in these bodies, with these unique sets of experiences, and for the span of our particular lifetime.

"We are not human beings who have occasional spiritual experiences; we are spiritual beings having an occasional human experience."

Look into the eyes of a newborn baby and you'll see that as human beings, we really are comprised far more of consciousness than we are of matter. We are born into the world innocent, trusting, and completely devoid of preconceptions or limiting beliefs. The people and things that exist around us occur to us as extensions of ourselves. After all, the moment we express a need, someone or something usually comes along to meet it. In our natural state, we experience and express the full range of our human emotions without restriction, pretense, or even a shred of self-consciousness. As babies, the question of whether we are worthy of love or of having our needs met doesn't even exist. We come in hardwired with the knowledge that the world is abundant, that we too are abundant, and that we are of course deserving of having all of our desires fulfilled. We don't hesitate to voice our discontent when our needs are not getting met, and we certainly don't pretend to be happy when we're not. Before we are taught to seek approval and validation outside of ourselves, we inherently understand that the inner world of our own thoughts, feelings, perceptions and desires – not the external world of people, things and possessions – is primary to our well-being. The way we feel is far more important to us than what we have, what we do, or how we look.

Somewhere around the time of our first or second birthday, language infiltrates our world, giving definition and form to what was previously formless and undefined. From our parents and other elders we are given distinctions about the objects that exist around us ("This is a chair." "This is blue."), and we're even given distinctions about who we are and how we should behave ("You're Mama's good girl." "Wave bye-bye to Daddy."). Suddenly, the world is no longer a natural extension of ourselves which we are free to interact with, play with and create with, but a material, external reality that we must learn to manipulate in order to get our needs met. The world now exists "out there," while we exist "in here," and the experiences we crave, such as happiness, contentment, joy, love and freedom are seen as originating from sources outside of ourselves, and these we must seek out and possess in order to attain.

To affect a change in the way we feel inside, we are taught that we must affect a change in the world around us. If we ever have an inner sense of feeling frustrated, unhappy or discontent, we look to others outside ourselves, and we carry it longingly into adulthood. "What I need is a new boyfriend," we decide, "and then I'll be happy." Or, "If only I made more money (or had a baby, or lost 10 pounds, or had a second home where I can be near the water)..." This original fallacy in our thinking – this "outside-in" approach to happiness – sets us on a lifelong journey toward a destination that we can never reach.

Anytime we are looking outside ourselves for an experience that can only be generated from within – such as approval, recognition, acceptance or love – we are coming from a mindset of lack and nothing and no one will ever be enough to fill that void. The new lover might initially do the trick, but then suddenly he just isn't showing up the way he once did, or the success we thought for sure would finally prove that we are deserving of love ends up occurring like a "Now what?" phenomenon. Even big goals that we've had for a long time often don't bring us the fulfillment we thought they would.

Anytime we are looking outside ourselves for an
experience that can only be generated from within –
such as approval, recognition, acceptance or love –
we are coming from a mindset of lack.

Ever since the beginning of my career as a teacher and a coach, one of my big goals was to become a *New York Times* bestselling author and have my work featured on national TV. This was the biggie for me, because I felt the accomplishment of it represented a milestone that would cause my life to dramatically change for the better – and I had already created an amazing life. When I got the call from my literary agent that my third book had hit the list at #5, I was initially so excited. I happened to be at the mall with my two young boys who were almost three and a year and a half at the time. I kneeled down to them in their double stroller and said, "Mommy is a *New York Times* bestselling author." They looked at me like I was speaking a foreign language. It didn't make them love me any more than they already did. It didn't make my husband change the way he looked at me or how much he loved me, because he already loved me for me, not for what I accomplished.

After about a day of celebrating the milestone I'd worked toward for years, I actually started to feel depressed. Here I was, finally a *New York Times* bestselling author who had appeared on the *Today* show and many other national TV spots, and my life had not changed overnight the way I had imagined it would. In fact, my life was exactly the same as it was before. The accomplishment of my new title did not meet the expectations that I had, and I felt really deflated. Yes, doing TV appearances was fun, and yes, having the title of "bestselling author" gave me more credibility in the eyes of other people, but for me inside it didn't do a thing. If anything, I actually felt less fulfilled, because if THAT didn't do it, then what would?

Searching for external things that we hope will make us feel good inside is the cause of much of our unhappiness. This outside-in approach to happiness disconnects us from the true source of our creative power and takes us further away from the essence of how we want our lives to look and feel. Manifestation is not about creating from the outside in, like many of us were taught. It's not the experiences, people, or things we desire that bring us the joy. It is the joy that brings us the experiences, people and things we desire. On one hand, running after all these things trying to accomplish what I have was great, but on the other hand, the "things" I have created were never what I was really seeking. Although it was disguised as a goal to become a *New York Times* bestselling author, what I was actually seeking was my own connection to myself and to the energy of feeling full.

Everything that exists in the outer world of form – including all living beings and all inanimate objects, like the book you are holding in your hands – is energy. Can you feel it?? So too, the inner world of our thoughts, feelings, perceptions, desires and beliefs is also made up of energy. Take a moment to close your eyes and see if you can feel the energy that is pulsating throughout your body. You are literally made up of energy. All energy generates an electromagnetic field which vibrates at a particular frequency, and this vibration can be felt, even if it can't be seen. Our own particular vibration is transmitted through the airwaves like a radio signal, and is registered by everyone and everything around us. In the same way that a magnet is attractive to steel, we draw into our lives energy that resonates at a similar frequency to our own.

The people, situations and experiences that come into our lives are always a perfect vibrational match to the frequency that we are sending out through the actions we take, the words we speak, and most significantly, through the thoughts, beliefs, conclusions, perceptions and feelings that we dwell on in the privacy of our own hearts and minds. Even if we never voice them, they are silently but powerfully conveyed to all-that-is, because the universe we live in reads and responds not to our words, but to our vibration. All that we manifest and don't manifest into our lives is governed by this process of attraction.

In the same way that a magnet is attractive to steel, we draw into our lives energy that resonates at a similar frequency to our own.

The Law of Attraction

The phenomenon that we now define as the Law of Attraction is far from new. In fact, this universal law has been written about and passed down throughout the ages by countless teachers and wisdom traditions. When Buddha made the observation that "As a man thinketh, so he becomes," he was conveying the essence of this powerful law. Even the Golden Rule, which advises us to "Do unto others as we would have others do unto us" is a testament to the basic understanding that what we send out eventually comes back. Whatever we are focused upon, within the invisible realm of our thoughts, eventually manifests into outer form. The Law of Attraction arises from the understanding that because the universe we live in is energetically based, whatever energy we generate from within is joined by (or attracted to) energies that are of an equal frequency, resonance, or vibration. The state of everything in our external world – our bodies, our relationships, our finances – is a direct reflection of our internal state. In the simplest terms, the Law of Attraction is merely the principle that "Like attracts like." This law is universal, meaning it works for everyone, all the time, whether we are aware of it or not. Just like the law of gravity, once we understand how it works, we can stop fighting against it and start using it to our benefit.

The Law of Attraction is universal, meaning it works for everyone, all the time, whether we are aware of it or not.

Right now, as you read these words, you are generating a particular vibration in relation to every aspect of your life that is important to you. As human beings, we can't *not* do this. Our thoughts are creative. Whether we are aware of it or not, we are continually responding to our environment and clarifying our preferences about what we want and don't want – in the same way we select a dress from a clothing rack or decide what to order for lunch after scanning a menu. What we may not realize, however, is that the universe is always listening – not to our words but to our energy. Through the vibration we offer in relation to our *it* and our *all*, we actually establish an energetic relationship with the very people, circumstances, events and experiences that we desire to draw into our lives. You already have a relationship with the abundance you desire. You have a relationship with the level of health and vitality you want to experience. You have a relationship with the intimate partner or the friends or adventure or fun that you want to magnetize into your life. The question to ask yourself is, "What is the quality of those relationships?" The lower your vibration, the more you are resisting, and therefore hindering, the process. The higher your vibration when you contemplate the outcomes you desire, the more attractive you become to them, and the faster and more fluidly they manifest. As speaker Harrison Klein explains, "Once you decide what it is that you want and begin to vibrate from that place, you absorb and internalize the feeling of already having manifested it. The rest is just watching it show up."

"Once you decide what it is that you want and begin to vibrate from that place, you absorb and internalize the feeling of already having manifested it. The rest is just watching it show up."

To find out whether the vibration we are sending out is attracting or repelling the *it* and the *all* that we desire, we need only to pay attention to the way we feel because our emotions are like guideposts which tell us whether the vibration we are emitting in each changing moment is in alignment with the expanded or the contracted version of ourselves. Generally speaking, when we feel good, we are in an energy field of abundance. When we feel bad, we are in an energy field of lack. The better we feel, the more allowing and receptive we are in relation to our desires; the worse we feel, the more resistance we are in and the harder they will be to attain. Emotions are simply energy in motion and like the keys on a piano, each one vibrates at a particular frequency.

The notion that different emotional states transmit different frequencies of vibration has been around for a long time. Scientology's L. Ron Hubbard introduced the idea in 1951, when he created an emotional tone scale intended to assess how "alive" or "dead" someone is in a spiritual sense. Fifty years later, psychiatrist David Hawkins' book *Power vs. Force* published the results of thousands of studies conducted using kinesiology, which classified the range of human emotions on a frequency scale of one to one thousand. More recently, Law of Attraction teachers Esther and Jerry Hicks developed what they call an Emotional Guidance Scale, which they shared in their 2005 book, *Ask and It Is Given*. As you read through this list, notice that the vibration generated by each emotional state feels progressively lower, slower, and more dense:

The Vibrational Range of Emotions:

1. Joy/Knowledge/Empowerment/Freedom/Love/Appreciation
2. Passion
3. Enthusiasm/Eagerness/Happiness
4. Positive Expectation/Belief
5. Optimism
6. Hopefulness
7. Contentment
8. Boredom
9. Pessimism
10. Frustration/Impatience/Irritation
11. Overwhelm
12. Disappointment
13. Doubt
14. Worry
15. Blame
16. Discouragement
17. Anger
18. Revenge
19. Hatred/Rage
20. Jealousy
21. Insecurity/Guilt/Unworthiness
22. Fear/Grief/Depression/Despair/Powerlessness

Once you've become practiced at the art of paying attention to the emotional and vibrational frequency you are sending out, this list will be extremely useful to you – as it has been to me – in helping you raise the frequency you are sending out. In the beginning, as you're learning to become more attuned to your own emotions, it can be useful to think of your range of emotional states in simpler terms. Karen Lamark Wilson, an amazing energy worker and my longtime coach, once shared with me that there are really only five basic emotions that we as human beings can experience: *glad, mad, sad, fear* and *shame*. Out of a combination of each of these primary feeling states, a multitude of other emotional responses are possible, each one expressing a slightly different sensation or nuance: The range of emotions that fall within the vibrational frequency of *glad* are those that cause us to feel good, powerful, positive and receptive. Joy, empowerment, freedom, love, appreciation, passion, anticipation, optimism, hopefulness and contentment are all different expressions of the emotional state known as *glad*. *Mad* emotions are those we experience when we are in a state of resistance. Frustration, pessimism, impatience, irritation, overwhelm, revenge, hatred and rage are examples of the types of emotions we may experience when we are feeling *mad*. Disappointment, discourage-ment, boredom, grief, despair, depression and powerlessness are all within the vibrational range of *sad* emotions, while doubt, worry, and insecurity fall within the range of *fear*. And finally, feelings of guilt, remorse, embarrass-ment or unworthiness are expressions of *shame*.

The idea here is that higher emotions generate a higher vibrational field, and the higher our vibrational field, the faster, easier and more spontaneously our *it* and *all* gets drawn into our experience. When you're experiencing high vibrating emotions such as passion, empowerment, freedom and appreciation, the vibration you're sending out is consistent with abundance, *and* you're in a state of non-resistance. In this state, you magnetize what you want effortlessly and joyfully. Good luck seems to follow you wherever you go, resources reveal themselves around every corner, and obstacles either rarely arise or are easily overcome.

Lower, slower emotions, on the other hand – fear, overwhelm, competition or self-doubt – are indications that we are emitting a vibration that is consistent with scarcity, lack, and resistance. This vibration is then matched by the Law of Attraction, bringing us situations, people, circumstances and events that elicit from us more of the same. If you've ever been completely frustrated with something, for example, you know that the vibration of frustration seems to act like an invisible magnet that seeks out and finds any and all possible events and scenarios that contribute to more frustration. We've all had one of those days when we allow something to trigger a downward spiral: You stub your toe. There's a snowstorm on the day you have a long commute. Your children aren't listening to you. Your pants don't button the way they did last week. The Starbucks girl is totally rude – and on and on it goes. Not only are you not experiencing your *it* and *all,* but everything feels like an uphill battle, and the more effort you apply, the more likely you are to end up creating more of what you don't want rather than more of what you do.

The higher our vibrational field, the faster, easier and more spontaneously our it and all gets drawn into our experience.

The days when you seem to hit every red light, when nothing comes easily and when you just feel "off" – as well as the days when doors magically seem to open, results come easily, and you look and feel fantastic – do *not* happen by accident. They happen as a result of the vibration we are generating from within, because it is our vibration that is matched and reflected back to us by everyone and everything. Becoming aware of and responsive to the information we are receiving from within, from our own emotions, is essential to becoming the kind of woman who elicits cooperation and support wherever she goes; the kind of woman for whom things always seem to work out, and who attracts what she wants without a lot of drama or struggle. The secret to becoming a woman who creates external success, while maintaining an internal sense of ease and fluidity, lies in learning to read and respond to what we are creating in our inner world *before* it manifests externally.

Being a woman with the "it" factor, who routinely finds herself in the "right place at the right time" is not a function of luck, nor of coincidence, good karma, destiny or fate. It is the result of systematically re-training ourselves to stay attuned to our own internal guidance system – rather than habitually tuning in to the needs of others – so we can receive the early, subtle clues sent to us by our emotional guidance system. Learning to redirect our focus within is a skill that has to be developed and one that requires continued practice, because it flies in the face of how most of us were taught to relate to the world. But this is the only way we can develop awareness as to when something feels right, and choose to take that action, and knowing when something feels wrong and choosing *not* to take the action. Only by tuning in to our own energy are we able to recognize the path that will align us with our *it* and our *all*. In my recent conversation with Harrison Klein, he explains this process as "using your entire body to experience life as opposed to trying to process it as a mental thing." I love this description because manifestation does *not* occur at the level of the mind – visualizing what we want is only the very first step of the process. It occurs at an energetic level. Once you develop the skill of reading the energy around you rather than simply listening to your thoughts about what is happening around you, this awareness becomes an inner compass that you take with you into every aspect of your life and each new situation.

> *"Use your entire body to experience life*
> *as opposed to trying to process it as a mental thing."*

The more in tune we become with our own energy field, the more we're able to sense ourselves from within. We carry with us the knowledge that we're fabulous, that we're important, and that we're deserving of manifest-ing all our desires with ease. When things aren't turning out the way we'd like and we lose our balance, we know how to regain it – not by demanding others to change, but by making the energetic adjustment within ourselves. This inner knowing radiates out from us like an aura, making us much less reliant on others to validate us, and far less attached to people or things showing up in any particular way. The more masterful we become at working with our energy, the better we are able to disengage from emotional patterns with others who no longer serve us – even those who are long-standing or highly charged. A quick case in point from my own life:

Although my mother-in-law, Nicole, and I now enjoy a very honest and cooperative relationship, early on, a string of incidents and misunderstand-ings created a lot of strain between us, and within the family as a whole. All of these incidents, I later realized, were the result of decisions we had made about each other – solidified again and again in our interactions over several years – and which we had each come to relate to as "the truth" about the other person. Of course I couldn't see this at the time, because I was not only attached to the way I perceived Nicole, but felt justified in my percep-tion. The tension between us began one year when Frederic and I were newly married and I was planning a birthday party for him. Nicole wanted to know if she could do anything to help, so I thanked her and asked her if she would please pick up the cake since the bakery would be on her way to our house. She agreed, and also offered to bring some salads and snacks so I wouldn't have to make another trip to the store. When she arrived at the party two hours late with no explanation or apology, I felt resentful and angry. When she complained to Frederic that I had asked a 60-year-old woman to run all over town picking up cakes, I initially felt betrayed, and then infuriated. Unable to contain my emotions, I left the party, sat inside my car which was parked in the garage, and called my mother. As I was ranting to my mom about Nicole's behavior – and using plenty of choice words to make my case – I glanced in the rear view mirror and saw Nicole standing there. She heard everything I had just said. Of course, this only heightened the mutual mistrust and resentment between us.

Although I made several attempts to heal the situation and improve our relationship, we invariably wound up in more misunderstandings that created even more ill will and hurt feelings. Eventually I came to the conclusion that it was safer to do everything myself than to risk depending on someone else and being disappointed when they didn't come through. Far from being made from a clear frame of mind, that decision was laced with a clear, strong vibration of resentment – which of course ensured that I would attract into my relationship with Nicole more things to feel resentful about.

Sure enough, this same dynamic was re-enacted soon after our son Alex was born. Frederic had asked Nicole to come to the house one day to take care of him so I could get some work done. I waited and waited, but she never showed up. When Frederic called his mom to find out what had happened, she said that she didn't come over because I hadn't called her to confirm. I felt a powerful surge of the anger, resentment and frustration that was seething just under the surface. My perception now was that not only could I not rely on her or count on her in any way, but even worse, I felt like a victim of her behavior. I started to dread family get-togethers, and even the thought of spending time with her would send my vibrational set point plummeting. Often, when we were planning an event with my husband's side of the family, I would actually become physically sick.

As a way of managing the situation and trying to keep the hostility between us from escalating, I learned to set boundaries and limit the time I spent with her. But this was not a solution, only a Band-Aid and a distraction tactic. In fact, I was so upset about what had happened in the past, and so committed to my point of view that she could not be counted on, that I had no space inside for her to show up any differently. Anger was my dominant emotional set point in relation to her, and it took very little to set me off.

Simultaneous to all of this, Nicole had come to her own conclusions when it came to the way she perceived and related to me, and these conclusions also impacted the emotional set point of our relationship. In the midst of the upset between us at Frederic's birthday party, I had (consciously or unconsciously) passed her over when asking everyone if they wanted something to drink. This imprinted firmly in her mind and she began to see me as being inattentive to her and inconsiderate of her needs. Although in all the subsequent times that she came to our house, I made a mental note to offer her something to eat or drink, I would sometimes get distracted with cooking or with one of the boys, and forget. There was nothing intentional about my behavior, but Nicole perceived me as being insensitive, and as ignoring her in particular. If we were passing bread around the dinner table and I failed to offer her a slice, she would have the experience of being passed over. At one event, she was literally the only guest who was not asked if she wanted something to drink. It was not our intention to ignore anyone, but it made sense to me that if anyone would have the experience of being ignored, it would be Nicole. She was attracting that behavior from both my husband and myself; because that is what she expected of us, and so that is how we had to show up. I had to laugh at this, because it is so uncharacteristic of either of us. To say the least, the tension between Nicole and me was palpable, and anytime we were in the same room together, we pushed each other's buttons. I evoked anger in her, and she evoked anger in me.

One Mother's Day she came to our house for a brunch to celebrate all the mothers in our family – her, myself and also my sister-in-law who had just had a baby. When Nicole arrived, she took my children aside and told them that it was her day, and they were to celebrate her. This time, instead of blaming her for my emotions, I allowed myself to feel them, and – more importantly – to receive the message that they were trying to send me. Without anger, I was able to communicate to Nicole that this was Mother's Day – a day for her to be celebrated by her children, my day to be celebrated by mine, and our day to celebrate together. Immediately after expressing my emotions, I felt the anger release. It was a good start.

A week later, I was planning another party – this time for my son – and was feeling anxious about seeing her. And then it occurred to me that I was projecting my fears about the past into the future, and in so doing was writing a script for a role I had no interest in playing. I reminded myself that I have the power to decide how I want my relationship with my mother-in-law to be. It is up to me, I told myself. I will create it the way I intend it, and what I send out will come back to me. I then realized that I was still holding onto anger from long ago. I was tired of it; I had outgrown it, and I was ready to let it go. I then asked myself, "What would I have to give up in order to shift my emotional set point with Nicole?" Almost immediately I heard that I would have to give up being a victim. I would have to release my past anger. I would have to invite gratitude into the places within me where resentment used to live. I decided then and there that this was the outcome I wanted – this was me *having it all* in relation to my family. I was committed to releasing the past and willing to walk into the relationship brand new.

I deliberately shifted my emotional energy from anger and judgment to hope and acceptance. I stopped focusing on her and pulled all my attention back to myself and decided to enjoy myself. I reminded myself that I was not responsible for her or her happiness. I told myself that it's okay to choose not to rely on her for help, because I don't want to be disappointed, but that I don't have to make this choice while carrying the energy of anger with me anymore. She had asked me on Mother's Day if there was anything she could help with for Alex's upcoming party and I said, "Thank you. I have it covered." This time, my communication was clean, clear, and had no undertone of resentment.

At the end of the party, Nicole and I were standing shoulder-to-shoulder at the kitchen sink, and she was helping me clean up. In that moment, I felt genuine gratitude that she was by my side. I looked at her and thanked her for her help, and then I told her "I appreciate you, and I love you." She beamed and gave me a beautiful, heartfelt hug. She was so excited by this moment of connection that she screamed, "Quick, Jimmy, get the camera!" Nicole's husband, Jimmy, and Frederic both came into the kitchen. Frederic was clearly moved by the display of affection between his mom and me because he could see it was real and genuine. An entirely different energy now flowed between us. After he took the picture (visit www.TheArtOfHavingItAll.com to check it out), he walked over and embraced us both in his arms. His mom and his wife were no longer at war; instead we were actually appreciating and loving one another. As he walked away, I whispered to Nicole, "This is all he wants."

It's impossible to hold onto anger, resentment and righteousness in the present and expect to create anything other than that in our future. Whatever we are feeling in the inner world of our thoughts and emotions is literally a "coming attraction" of what is in the process of manifesting in the outer world of form. If we are holding onto blame or feeling anxious or fearful, it is because we are projecting that something unwanted is going to happen in the future; something which we feel we have no ability to change. We might feel doubtful that we'll ever meet the partner we think will finally make us happy. Or maybe we're scared of losing the job that we love. Maybe we're afraid that we'll never get out of debt because we owe so much money.

The lack of connection to a happier future creates negative feelings in our now. So too, if we are still connected to some unresolved guilt, sadness or resentment from our past, those emotions will continue to feed both our present and our future.

There's a principle in quantum physics which states that "All time is simultaneous." What this means is that unless we consciously release them, all emotions from our past – positive and negative – will remain part of our energetic point of attraction, influencing both the present moment and determining the future we are in the process of creating. How do we know when the past is having a negative impact on our present – and therefore our future? It's not necessary to delve endlessly into childhood memories, or to scrutinize our insecurities or shortcomings. In fact, dwelling too much on the past or getting caught up in what psychologists call "analysis paralysis" can become an addiction in itself and an obstacle to moving forward. The only time the past becomes relevant is when it's affecting our ability to create in the present. We know this is happening by a) the way we feel, and b) by the outcomes we produce. If we encounter the same types of obstacles again and again, or if something in present time triggers old emotions or brings back memories that are still unaddressed or unhealed, these are indications that we are transmitting vibrations in our now, that are rooted in the past. By releasing this old energy, we change our current vibrational set point and create a clearing for new possibilities to arise.

There exists no preordained future for any of us. Instead, we all have thousands of possible future selves – any one of which can be brought to life through the power of our focus. As long as we are unaware of the influence that the past has on our present, we remain powerless to change it, and find ourselves instead wondering why we continue to create more of the same. But as deliberate creators, we can design any future we desire by releasing unwanted emotional energy from the past and consciously replacing it with the quality of energy that we *do* want to permeate our lives. This one shift ushers in a new vibrational set point and therefore an entirely new future experience.

We all have thousands of possible future selves – any one of which can be brought to life through the power of our focus.

By connecting with the *it* and *all* that we desire and establishing an energetic relationship with it, we are deliberately living into that future experience, rather than simply reliving the past. When we are energetically connected with and living into a bright and happy future where everything works out for us ("The future's so bright, ya gotta wear shades!"), we are in the process of magnetizing that bright future to us. How do we know? Because we feel good! By paying attention to your emotions and interpreting their vibrational content, you can both discover the frequency you are sending out, and you can alter that frequency. Nothing can happen until you start paying attention to you, and this means listening to your emotions rather than trying to resist, suppress, ignore or deny them.

> *Nothing can happen until you start paying attention to you,*
> *and this means listening to your emotions rather than*
> *trying to resist, suppress, ignore or deny them.*

What most people don't understand is that when we cut ourselves off from feeling lower-level or "negative" emotions, we are also cutting ourselves off from feeling high vibrating "positive" emotions as well. If we're busy repressing anger or resentment, we lose our ability to experience passion, love and excitement for life too. If we suppress one, we suppress them all. And since we live in a universe where the vibration we send out forms the energetic relationship between ourselves and what we desire, it's essential that we get real and honest with ourselves about the vibrations we are truly giving off. In other words, we have to allow ourselves to feel.

Feeling the full range of our emotions is something that comes completely natural to us when we're younger – that is, until we are told that "Little girls shouldn't be angry," or to "Stop crying, or I'll give you something to cry about." Many of us disconnected from our emotions just to survive; to feel them would be to risk becoming completely overwhelmed, or it would be terrifying. And of course, the longer we have been cut off from our emotions, the more terrifying it can be to face the prospect of actually feeling ourselves again – trust me, I know this from personal experience. I was a smoker for sixteen years; dabbled in recreational drugs when I was younger; shopped until my credit cards were so maxed out that I had to take out a loan from my grandfather; sought the attention of men that were not good for me, and even put up with relationships where I was being taken advantage of – all in an attempt not to feel what was really going on inside me. My pattern was to seek self-acceptance by trying to make myself into what others wanted me to be. Instead of being informed by my emotions and being real and honest in the moment about *how* I was feeling, I would suppress my emotions until they reached a boiling point, because to feel them in the moment as I experienced them was beyond scary; it was paralyzing. So rather than express my anger and resentment as they arose, I let them build up until I could no longer contain it. I would then blow up and release them in dramatic, and sometimes inappropriate, ways.

> *My pattern was to seek self-acceptance by trying to make myself into what others wanted me to be.*

When I first started psychotherapy – and later, when I began learning about and working with energy – I had a lot of resistance to reconnecting with and feeling my emotions. I actually thought I was going to die if I allowed them to come to the surface, because they were so intense. I had been repressing them for so long that I really had no idea if I could survive the effect they would have, not only on me but those around me as well. What I discovered is that allowing the full range of our emotions is synonymous with allowing all of ourselves, and with stepping into the fullness of who we are. Our emotions are far more powerful than our thoughts or words. They are the strongest points of attraction we have, and we will receive back whatever we are asking for through our vibration, whether it is wanted or not. If we don't give ourselves permission to feel our feelings, how can we possibly know what vibration we are emitting? The ability to feel our emotions is the launching point for being able to feel and work with energy – and developing the ability to work with energy is the key to magnetizing all that we want to manifest in our lives.

When I interviewed Dr. Symeon Rodger, "The Warrior Coach," for this book, he shared with me a beautiful Native American practice of imagining oneself as a hollow bone. "There is a unique connection between the energy within us and the energy around us. To feel ourselves as a hollow bone is to become a conduit for that energy. We can then stop trying to figure it all out and relax into it." When our emotions flow without resistance, our body-mind vessel is free to become the instrument it was always intended to be. We are energy generators – like living, breathing, *feeling* radio towers – and the signal we send out is the place of origin for everything that gets magnetized back into our lives. When this signal is unfettered by the past, it is clear, resonant and powerful; it moves fast and free to bring into existence the future we desire. The more sensitive and receptive we become to the moment-to-moment communications being delivered to us by our emotions, the more we allow them to inform us. If we are "checked out" from our emotions or unwilling to receive them when they arise, we deprive ourselves of the ability to respond to each moment creatively and resourcefully.

Because my life's work is literally founded on the wisdom of viewing emotions as energetic guides, I'm usually pretty aware of my feelings as they shift from moment-to-moment. I had an experience recently, however, that caught me completely off guard and showed me how my resistance to feeling a particular emotion (in this case, fear) placed my children and me in harm's way.

After a great afternoon of sightseeing in Chicago, my boys and I had just arrived back at our hotel to relax. Filled with guests and staff, the hotel lobby was a flurry of activity. The elevator door opened and Alex, Maxim and I got in. When a man walked onto the elevator immediately after us, I noticed that he was tall and big, and that his clothing and appearance didn't seem consistent with someone who would stay at a 5-star hotel in downtown Chicago. Shortly behind him another man, who had a similar build and appearance as the first man, stepped inside.

Fear would have been the appropriate emotion for me to feel in response to this situation. Clearly, a woman – with two young children, and arms loaded with a purse and shopping bags – alone in an elevator with two suspicious looking men is at a great disadvantage. Had I allowed myself to feel the emotion of fear that was being generated within me, I could have used that energy to guide me in one of a dozen different directions, all of which would have guaranteed our safety. In that moment, however, I was not allowing myself to experience the emotion of fear, and as a result, I had no access to the information it held for me. Disconnected from my emotions and therefore my guidance system, I froze, aware only of the mental chatter in my head.

Thankfully, at the very last moment before the elevator doors closed, a tall young man stepped inside, blocking the door from closing, and told both men to get out of the elevator. After they got out of the elevator, he got in and pressed the button for floor number three. When the door closed, the young man turned to me and said, "You were a target. Those men were not guests of the hotel. They were going to rob you. I am a bellman here, and I've seen them before." The doors opened and as he was getting out he said, "My name is Marcus." And the doors closed. He came and went like Batman, leaving me standing in the elevator with my two boys in a state of total shock.

The situation I attracted in the elevator that day was a perfect match to my internal state of being. Up until that point in my life, I had been deeply afraid to allow myself to feel fear, so I would suppress it, or distract from it, or talk myself out of it anytime this emotion would arise. But the universe doesn't respond to our distraction mechanisms or rationalizations; it responds to our energy. Fear was the energy I was sending out, and what I received in return was an encounter that evoked fear in me. I share this story as a way to underscore the fact that the Law of Attraction does not discriminate. It magnetizes to us more of whatever vibration we are already emitting – consciously or unconsciously. The good news is that the more willing we become to allow and listen to our emotions, the more deliberate we can become about the vibration we are offering.

Everything is a reflection of your vibration, and you are the originator of the vibration you send out. Once you understand that, your power to magnetize grows exponentially: You magnetize more abundance. You generate more ideas and new possibilities. And you draw people into your experience – employers, employees, publishers, assistants… you name it – who have the exact resources needed to bring those ideas to fruition in your life. It all starts with the signal you're sending out. It all starts with YOU. Shifting the internal energy that you bring to any situation is the key to becoming a powerful creator in every situation. The inner creates the outer; this is the secret to deliberate manifestation, and to creating your *it* and your *all*. By aligning the vibration of your dominant emotions with the essence of what you desire, you not only magnetize the outer results you want, but – more importantly – you also open yourself up to receive the inner fulfillment that comes from creating them.

— ● —

PLAY SHEET FOR CHAPTER 3:
Creation from the Inside Out

Identify a specific area in your life – your finances, your career, relationships with others, for example – where you feel discontent, frustrated or unfulfilled; an aspect of your life where you do not yet feel you have it all.

As you contemplate the current condition of this part of your life and your relationships with the people involved in it, see if you can identify the dominant emotion or vibration that you are emitting in response to it. Do you feel resentment? Disappointment? Resignation? Allow yourself to feel this emotion in your body. Where is the feeling located? How large of an area does it cover?

As you connect with this emotion, notice if it is familiar to you. Thinking back to the past, are there other relationships or circumstances in which you have also experienced it? Notice the feelings in your body as you consider this.

Acknowledge that *you* – not any other person from your present or your past – are the sole generator of your vibration, and allow yourself to see if there is anything you would have to give up in order to shift your vibration in relation to this situation. Would you need to release some old resentment? Would you have to give up being a victim? Would you have to let go of being right? As you identify what you have been holding on to, see if you can become willing to give it up, and notice what happens to your vibration as you do.

As you liberate this outdated vibration from your energy field, allow yourself to connect with the feeling you want to experience instead. What does your *it* and *all* feel like in this aspect of your life? Breathe in this higher vibration, imagining it filling all the spaces in your body and mind where the old emotion used to live, and allowing it to become your new point of attraction.

CHAPTER **4:**
Opening to Receive: How to Reset Your "Allowing" Meter

Once a new desire has been born within us, there are only two basic positions we can take in relation to that desire: we can resist its manifestation into our lives, or we can allow it – and therefore magnetize it – into being. Allowing is our natural state. It's the way we're all born when we enter the world – pliable, receptive, deserving, and open to every possible expression of well-being, abundance and joy. In its free and unobstructed state, our body-mind system is in direct connection and communion with the unlimited energy and inspiration of the universe; it flows through us like water rushes through an open pipe. Resistance, on the other hand, is a conditioned response; a pattern of thinking, feeling and behaving which can become so habitual that it sometimes seems to occur as an automatic reflex. Resistance is rooted in a belief in insufficiency and a fear of lack. It is the act of steeling ourselves against dangers, real or imagined, all the while justifying our defensive stance. Ironically, the more energy we expend to make the case that our guardedness is necessary, the more things we draw into our experience to guard ourselves against. While it's true that the universe is infinitely abundant, it's also true that we can only receive as much of that abundance as we are willing to allow – and we are the only ones who can determine that. As Marianne Williamson, an internationally acclaimed spiritual teacher, explains, "From a spiritual perspective, having and being are the same thing. You can *have* whatever you allow yourself to *be*."

When Albert Einstein asserted that "The most important decision we make is whether we believe we live in a friendly or hostile universe," he was suggesting that what we determine to be true for ourselves is what we will experience. The good news is that you never need to wonder whether you are in a state of allowing (and magnetizing toward you) or a state of resisting (and pushing away from you) in relation to your *it* and your *all,* because as with all things, your emotions are your guide.

> *"From a spiritual perspective, having and being are the same thing.
> You can have whatever you allow yourself to be."*

Resistance always brings with it a feeling of constriction. Physically, your stomach may become tight; your breathing shallow; your jaw or shoulders tense. Mentally, your thoughts tend to revolve around concerns, constraints, problems or limitations. Emotionally, you might feel stressed out, discouraged, fearful, doubtful or otherwise ill at ease. Any time you are experiencing these lower-level (and notice here that I am calling them "lower-level" emotions, not "bad" emotions, because all of our emotions exist to guide us) emotions, you are in resistance. These emotions arise in us for the purpose of informing us and letting us know that we are off course or that we need to pay attention to something, because the vibration we are sending out is not in alignment with the current evolution of our own desire.

When the situation we find ourselves in opposes something we want or hold dear, we instinctively register this discord in our bodies as a restriction of freedom. The essence of who we are is limitless and unbounded, and when something manifests in our experience that is contrary to this, our high, fast-moving thoughts and feelings grind to a screeching halt. In an attempt to get ourselves back into alignment, many of us make a grave error in perception: We blame our discomfort on something or someone outside of ourselves – and then focus our attention in trying to change that external condition in order to feel better within ourselves. Although we rarely realize this at the moment we're doing it, anytime we take a stand against what is happening in the moment, we actually become energetic proponents of the very conditions we want to change. Remember, what we focus on expands. Anytime we are in resistance – and whether it's justifiable or not – we are literally repelling the manifestation of our desires. Instead of using the powerful Law of Attraction to our benefit, we are using it against ourselves by magnetizing more of what we don't want than what we do.

Because resistant thoughts and feelings move at a much lower, slower frequency than the allowing, expansive nature of our desires, they temporarily obstruct the flow of abundance to our body-mind system, like a blockage in a pipe. That's why they are so painful to feel. In those moments when our outer experience is not a match to our inner desires, what is called for is not resistance, but acceptance.

In everyday terms, if you're driving along and realize that you took a wrong turn on the way to your destination, you first have to soften your thinking and accept what has happened. In other words, you have to slow down the momentum before you can turn around. This is as simple as saying to yourself, *So I made a wrong turn – so what?* Rather than fighting against what has already happened in the past, we yield to and harmonize with the energy of what's happening now. The moment we accept ourselves and our situation exactly as it is, we feel relief. Acceptance of what is, right now in this moment, is the only doorway through which a bigger and brighter future can emerge. When we are trying to make what's happening different than it is; when we are "shoulding" on ourselves, others or even the universe; or when we are attached to creating a certain outcome according to our timelines and ideas, we actually become an obstruction to our own forward progress.

Acceptance of what is right now in this moment is the only doorway through which a bigger and brighter future can emerge.

Acceptance is the key to releasing the grip of resistance and the first step toward creating a turnaround in any area of life where we are manifesting conditions other than those we desire. Rather than struggling against what is happening in the moment (which, as Deepak Chopra notes in *The Seven Spiritual Laws of Success,* "is like struggling against the entire universe"), we yield to the energy of our resistance by allowing ourselves to feel it fully. Just in case you weren't sure, this is *not* what most of us do when we are hit with a whoosh of anger, disappointment, shame, fear, or any other low-level emotion. What most people do – because this is the way most of us were trained – is just about anything to avoid feeling uncomfortable feelings when they arise. Think about it: Throughout your early childhood conditioning, how many times did you hear things like "Don't speak to me in that tone of voice," or "There is nothing to be afraid of"? In essence, the message most of us received is that it's not okay to feel our emotions – and, therefore, it's not okay to feel ourselves. So we learned early on to do whatever we needed to do to suppress, ignore, and distance ourselves from our feelings – and ourselves.

To the extent that we do not have access to our feelings, we remain powerless to change them, and to be informed by them. Avoiding or suppressing our lower-level emotions may seem like a quick-fix solution, but in reality, it only invites them to persist. If you doubt this, just think back to the last time you tried *not* to feel sad, angry or afraid and you'll realize that resistance simply doesn't work. We were meant to feel the full range of our emotions; they are our most powerful and insightful guides. If instead of trying to change the way we feel by numbing or distracting ourselves, we actually allow ourselves to feel and process them fully, in the moment they arise – without labeling them, explaining them, describing them, justifying them or judging them – they dissipate of their own volition and we experience a true and genuine release from that lower emotional state. What is left in the space of that negative emotion is ease, neutrality, and relief. From that more centered state of being, we are once again in a position to begin building momentum toward what is desired, rather than squandering our energy on resisting and complaining about what is not. By becoming present to what we are feeling, we take back some of our power to deliberately feel the way we want to. Let me give you an example:

A few years ago, I was consistently feeling used by a handful of differ-ent people in my life. My perception was that these people expected me to provide for them, both professionally and financially. At first this was just a source of mild irritation, but – unexpressed – it soon escalated into intense anger and frustration. Instead of paying attention to the information that my anger was trying to give me, I suppressed it. I ate lots of sugar, I shopped compulsively, and I would keep myself so hyped up on caffeine that I would be too busy running around doing things to actually feel.

My mentor, Karen, who had been trying for years to get me to slow down enough to feel my feelings and reconnect with myself, encouraged me to take the focus off of the people I felt were using me, and to pay closer attention to what was actually going on within me. Once I was able to be present enough with myself to tune into the energy of my emotions rather than pushing them away, I began to accept them and better understand them. I was feeling used, and this was causing me to feel angry. I then acknowledged that because I was unwilling to feel my own energy edges (or what some people call boundaries), I couldn't hear when my internal response to someone's request was a "No." Although I would have passionately denied it at the time, I was responsible for allowing people to use me. In saying "yes" to them, I left me and my "no" out of the equation. I was treating myself without regard or respect, and in so doing, I was training them how to treat me.

For the first time, I gave myself permission to feel the intensity of my anger – initially at the other people, but even more so at myself. As I breathed and allowed the anger to course through my body, all that I had been holding in for so long and pushing down like the proverbial beach ball under water came popping up, and all the pressure and frustration within me was released. When we allow ourselves to feel our uncomfortable feelings, I would later learn, they release naturally and easily.

It was at that point that I was able to forgive myself for not hearing my own "no," for not respecting my own "no," and for not communicating that "no" to others when that was how I was really feeling. It was not up to anyone else to hear, respect or listen to me; it was up to me. I was the one not listening to myself. They asked, and I said "yes," even though the answer inside of me was a "no." I kept giving and they kept taking – just as I had trained them to do. With that realization, I saw that there was no malicious intent on the part of anyone else. I was able to forgive those against whom I had been carrying a ton of anger and resentment, and I was also able to forgive myself.

From the new space created by the release of anger and forgiveness, I then made some new decisions. I decided that, for me, if something is even slightly a "no," it is still a NO, and it is up to me to accept that and to communicate it to others, even though my "no" might upset them. I had been so used to giving others what they wanted – because I so badly wanted to be liked, approved of or accepted by them – that I was cutting my own feelings out of the equation. In that moment, I decided that I was important, that what I felt was important, what I thought was important, and that honoring myself was important.

The outer dynamics of those relationships changed after that, but more significantly, I had learned how to relate to my emotions not as a part of me to be denied or controlled, but as powerful indicators of the vibration I was emitting in every moment. I learned that a big part of taking care of my emotional well-being is being willing to honor the natural signals my body sends me when something is a "yes" and when it is a "no," and communicating that in a way that is respectful of everyone concerned. Feeling our emotions is the key to learning to feel and direct vibration – and deliberately directing our vibration is the key to having it all.

Tuning in to Your It and Your All

The relationships, experiences, objects and circumstances that you have identified as being part of your *it* and your *all* do not need to be created. They already exist, right now in this moment as unmanifested possibilities that can be pulled into tangible existence at any time. Your *it* and *all* lives at a particular vibrational frequency, and in each and every moment, the vibration you are offering is either resonant with or dissonant with that frequency. Think of it like this: If you wanted to listen to coffeehouse rock on the radio, and knew that that type of music is broadcasted at the frequency set to 101.5 FM, you would turn your radio dial so that your receiver was set to pick up that frequency, right? Well, in the world of manifestation, YOU are a living, breathing, thinking, sensing, acting, feeling radio receiver, and whatever frequency you are dialed into is the frequency you receive. If your *it* and *all* is vibrating on 101.5 FM, but the receiver that is YOU is not lined up with that signal, there will be a big disconnect between what you're wanting and what you're getting. If your resistance is only minimal, you might still be able to hear the music, but the full clarity and richness of it will be distorted by static. If your resistance is so great that you are actually tuned into a different channel entirely (maybe you flipped to the insecurity channel, when what you want to feel is love), then instead of the coffeehouse rock you asked for, your receiver might be picking up sports radio or acid jazz.

Fortunately, there are only two steps to tuning out the frequency of what you don't want and tuning back in to the frequency that you do: The first step is to accept the fact that your receiver is currently resisting, or disallowing, the vibration you want to experience in relation to the subject you are focused upon – and here it's important to understand that acceptance is not the same thing as approval. We can accept something as being the way that it is, without necessarily agreeing with it. For example, I will never approve of the choice my sister made when she decided to end her own life, but after years of deep healing, I now accept it. I also don't approve when people become hyper-focused on negativity and see only what is lacking in their lives, but I no longer feel a need to change them. I simply accept that this is their perception at this moment in their lives, and their perception need not influence my own. Acceptance creates a feeling of freedom.

The second step is to begin to shift your vibration – either in tiny increments or in quantum leaps (both are possible). This process is what I call *Resetting Your Allowing Meter.* Learning how to shift your internal vibration from less resistance to greater allowing is the key not only to manifesting your future desires, but also to gaining more ease, contentment, neutrality and peace in the present moment. We all have the capacity to become masterful at resetting our Allowing Meter – after all, we did it effortlessly as children – but first, we have to learn how to read it.

Reading Your Allowing Meter

Just as a thermostat regulates the temperatures in our homes, the collective vibration we generate through our thoughts, beliefs, emotions, words and actions creates a very specific range of how much of all the things we desire we are actually in a position to receive. The vibration that we emit in each moment affects every aspect of our experience: what we notice and fail to notice, what we think and feel, and ultimately what we attract. The means for attaining something that we dearly want could be staring us square in the face, but if our vibration is not dialed into that frequency, it won't even land on our radar.

Your Allowing Meter is a lot like the inner mechanism that operates a thermostat: you set the temperature to whatever is comfortable to you – let's say 75 degrees. If the room gets too cold, the heating system is triggered to warm it back up. If it gets too hot, the heat shuts off and the air conditioner kicks on. The thermostat is simply responding to whatever set point you have predetermined, keeping you within just a few degrees of what you've decided – haphazardly or on purpose – is comfortable.

We all have physical set points – for example, our bodies are designed to keep our temperature right around 98.6 degrees – and I'm willing to bet that you're pretty clear about the set point needed to maintain your weight. For the most part, our physical set points are automatic. We don't have to will our body into sweating if we become too hot or to shiver when we become too cold. The body's mechanisms for keeping us in balance, or in a state of homeostasis, are natural, effortless and entirely automatic. Brilliant! Even more brilliant is that unlike our physical set points, our energetic set points are entirely under our control, and the more sensitive we become to reading them, the more fluidly we can shift them in order to bring about our desired result in each changing situation.

Our vibrational set point has an even greater influence on our overall well-being than our physical set points, because this is what defines the range of energies that we are able to register and respond to. Although you may not be consciously aware of it, you have distinct set points which determine just how much vitality, pleasure, ease, happiness, freedom, and abundance you are comfortable allowing into your life. In fact, you have a different vibrational set point for each different area – your finances, career, relationships, vitality... you name it. Venture too far in any direction from this set point of your Allowing Meter, and you will without a doubt experience some form of resistance or discomfort that lets you know that something is "off." Your Allowing Meter acts like an invisible rubber band around your waist – you can stretch only so far in the direction of what you desire before it snaps you back into the same place you are accustomed to being. Let's look at an everyday example of how this works:

Let's say that in relation to financial abundance, you have a set point of earning somewhere around $5,000 per month. This is your comfort zone, or – in energetic terms – your vibrational point of attraction regarding money. As long as you stay within a few hundred dollars of this amount, you feel comfortable. If one month, however, you bring in significantly less than $5,000, you would of course feel some discomfort in the form of a lower emotion – stress, anxiety, frustration, despair, fear, etc. Fueling this discomfort is resistance. You are energetically tuned in to the set point of $5,000 per month, and when you manifest something different from this, resistant thoughts and feelings arise to let you know. Again, you may have been conditioned to think of uncomfortable emotions as "negative," but in fact they are providing you with valuable information. They arise to let you know that in relation to your set point regarding abundance, *you* are out of alignment with *you*.

The same principle holds true for your weight, your self-image, the degree of ease or tension you experience in your relationships, and every other part of your life in which you have a certain expectation about the way you desire things to be. Even preferences as superficial as the cleanliness of your kitchen or how frequently you wash and wax your car all provide information about your current vibrational set point. When your internal set point is met and matched, you feel comfortable. When there is lack of alignment, you feel some degree of resistance. So far, so good – right? But this is where it gets even better.

While most of us have experienced the resistant thoughts and feelings that arise from not having *enough* money at the end of the month – to continue with our earlier example – what may be far less obvious is that our vibrational set point also kicks in when we manifest *more* than we are comfortable receiving. If your Allowing Meter is set to receive $5,000 per month and you come upon an unexpected windfall, chances are good that you will find a way to quickly relieve yourself of that extra cash. This phenomenon explains why most lottery winners soon find themselves in worse financial shape than they were before they won. Sure, they won the money, but because they didn't change their internal set point in relation to their finances, they quickly returned to the level of abundance that is comfortable for them. Our vibrational set points – in relation to every aspect of our lives that defines our *it* and our *all* – kick in just as fiercely, and sometimes even more so, when what we receive exceeds the amount that we have defined within the perimeters of our Allowing Meter. This, by the way, is the hidden mechanism that drives all acts of self-sabotage.

Self-Sabotage: How to Keep Yourself Safe – and Playing Small

If we try to expand our level of abundance without first expanding our ability to receive, we may succeed in the beginning, then unconsciously sabotage our results in order to keep ourselves in the range that feels good and familiar. Then, once our self-sabotage has taken us back down to our lowest vibrational set point, our Allowing Meter kicks in, we stop sabotaging, and start allowing in more abundance. These patterns of self-sabotage may manifest in one main area of our lives – we consistently create intense highs and lows in our finances, for example, or in our intimate relationships. One pattern I've seen with women in particular (and used to run myself) is that improvement in one area of life automatically triggers decline in another. So, if our marriage is happy and fulfilling, our finances start to suffer. To compensate, we apply extra effort to make our financial situation better – and then our relationships start to suffer. This is the drama to which many women have become deeply addicted. The belief that creating fulfillment in one area of life must involve sacrifice in another is a joy-robbing mindset that is epidemic in our culture – *especially* among women. To the extent we tell ourselves that we can't have it all, and that one aspect of our being must suffer in order for another to thrive, we keep ourselves bound to this cycle of self-sabotage.

Before I became skilled in the art of reading and resetting my vibrational set point, most areas of my life followed a predictable pattern of self-sabotage: I would manifest something great – an amazing new career opportunity – that would send my vibration soaring with the energy of joy and accomplishment. But because my energetic set point was still hovering somewhere between self-judgment and unworthiness, I was not able to allow myself to sustain this high vibration for any length of time. On some unconscious level, I'd start to say to myself, "Who am I to feel this joyful? Or "Why should things work out so easily for me?" After all, I was raised with the belief that hard work and sacrifice were the price that one has to pay for success.

So, inevitably, and quite unconsciously, I would do something that lowered my vibration. I'd eat something I didn't feel good about; I would go shopping and spend too much money; or – my favorite for a long time – I'd call my former husband, who would support me very quickly in abandoning my amazing mood and once again feeling horrible about myself and my life. The joy that I had longed to feel for so long and then created would then be replaced by my familiar pattern of beating myself up, because that was what I was used to doing within my own relationship with myself.

Early on in my relationship with Frederic, I felt undeserving of his adoration and love, to the point that it often felt uncomfortable to me. Rather than going to work within myself to become more allowing of love, I would look instead for ways to deflect it. I'd withdraw or start an argument, or become hyper-focused on any little imperfection. This was not a conscious, "Oh, I am experiencing more love from my husband than I am wired to receive, so I will focus on his nose hairs" kind of thing. I would see myself doing it, but couldn't figure out why I did it or how to change it. Because my vibration was more conditioned to resist than to receive, I would find a way to take myself out of the vibration of love and joy and back into more familiar territory. All of these patterns were a reflection of my being unable to allow *it all*. If we are used to beating ourselves up, deflecting our magnificence and light, or denying our connection to our fullness and power because it frightens us, we will continue to only let in what we are "comfortable" with. And we are the only ones who have the power to change this set point. Like a door that is locked from the inside, it can only be opened from within.

Sometimes our resistance to having it all is so subtle that we are the only ones who really know the ways in which we are depriving ourselves of happiness. To others, it may look like we have everything going for us, and yet we privately suffer because there is that "one area" where we just can't seem to find alignment or achieve our goals. It might show up as that extra body weight that diminishes our experience of worthiness or joy, or maybe we continually reenact some drama in the area of our intimate relationships that feeds our insecurities or keeps us always on edge. Scenarios like these are a reflection of our deep resistance to letting ourselves have it all and allowing ourselves to shine in all areas of our lives, all at once. We are multi-dimensional beings who seek full self-expression in every possible form, and to the extent we are limiting ourselves in one area, we limit ourselves in all.

It's relatively easy to *say* that you're committed to creating your life to reflect your unique vision of having it all, and it's even relatively easy to take external actions that lead you toward the fulfillment of that vision. The real work is what happens on the inside – in the relationship between you and you. Your willingness to rearrange the unseen landscape of your thoughts, beliefs, perceptions and emotions in order to allow yourself to receive whatever it is you're asking for is what creates the internal space for those external manifestations to take root. Their growth is nourished from within. As we release resistance, we expand our ability to receive, gently nudging doubt into possibility, unworthiness into self-compassion, guardedness into courage, and fear into trust.

The Law of Allowing

While ambition and effort are necessary for success, they represent only one part of the equation. To create our *it* and *all* in such a way that our success brings us contentment and fulfillment rather than overwhelm and stress, we must learn how to balance the energy of pushing forward and striving with the energy of yielding and allowing. The universal Law of Allowing is based on the understanding that all creation arises from this ebb and flow: The tide must recede in order to form into a wave. A seed is first pressed deep into dark rich soil before it begins its upward journey toward the sun. So too, getting what we *want* unfolds much more effortlessly and magically when we create it from a place of appreciating what we already *have*, whereas dwelling on the areas where we perceive there is a lack causes us to contract. When there is constriction, there can be no allowing. Is it possible to receive something when your hand is clenched tightly into a fist? No. To receive, our hand has to be open. What is true of our physical body is also true of our energy body. In order to allow more, we need to expand our container so there is space to take in more energy. The amazing author, speaker and singer/songwriter Rikka Zimmerman explains the process of opening the energy body as "imagining the inside of your body becoming more spacious, and expanding the outside edges of your being into the vibrational field of having it all." I love this, because it perfectly describes what it feels like to embody the Law of Allowing.

> *"Imagine the inside of your body becoming more spacious, and expanding the outside edges of your being into the vibrational field of having it all."*

Think about it: there is no such thing as "goal setting" in nature. Trees don't strive to reach a certain height. Air doesn't work to be drawn to and consumed by fire. Planet Earth doesn't clock in each day for another shift of orbiting the sun. How does the universe function, then, if not by hard work and willpower? It functions through the phenomenon of attraction and allowing. In the same way that plants are attracted to light and planets are magnetically pulled toward the sun, we have the power to magnetize into our lives all that we desire. This power hinges on our ability to *receive*, which is directly correlated to how much we are able to *allow*. What this means in practical terms is this: In the process of working toward a goal, we can remind ourselves that efforting, controlling and forcing do not have the power to bring us what we really want, because anything achieved through those means demands a sacrifice of intimacy, connection and balance. We might fulfill the goal, but at the cost of taxing an important relationship or even our own health. Allowing affects our relationship with ourselves, with others, and with the universe as a whole.

Inner Safety = Outer Progress

Before you can successfully take that next outer step toward greater abundance, you first have to allow yourself in the inner core of your being and nervous system to take that step – and this will require you to feel some degree of discomfort. It's just not possible to grow into more of who and what you want to become while remaining perfectly comfortable, because the moment you ask for more (and as long as you're alive and breathing, you will *always* ask for more), you trigger patterns of thought that tell you that you can't have it – in other words, you will encounter resistance. The solution doesn't lie in pushing yourself to take more and more external actions, but in learning to release the brakes that are holding you back from within. As author and speaker Lisa Nichols – who is one of the most captivating, passionate, and inspiring women I know – puts it, manifestation comes down to giving ourselves permission. "Give yourself permission to have," she explains. "Give yourself permission to be. Give yourself permission to need. Give yourself permission to let go." Having it all in the outer world begins with allowing ourselves to have it all within.

"Give yourself permission to have. Give yourself permission to be. Give yourself permission to need. Give yourself permission to let go."

Cultivating the inner knowing that it is safe to take the next step toward success is the very key that opens the door that allows more success into our lives. As we teach our nervous system, once exclusively committed to our survival, that it's safe for us to be as successful, as wildly abundant, as brilliant, and as outrageously happy as we desire to be, it drops all its defenses and eagerly and excitedly allows these experiences to come into our lives. When an outer opportunity arises, we meet it with an inner willingness to step up, charge ahead, and transform our intentions into reality. We have the ability to do this, regardless of whether our current circumstance is one of smooth sailing, or whether our efforts are being met with the inevitable obstacle along our path.

Bumps in the Road Do Not Mean Stop

Any bump in the road that we encounter on our way to fulfilling our desires has the potential to reflexively trigger a cascade of old thoughts, feelings and beliefs. It's as if we are literally passing through our past point of attraction on our way to our desired future. The more practiced we are at the old vibration, the easier and more tempting it will be to linger there. What's vital in those moments is to realize that you are being informed either by the future that you are choosing to call into being – a future in which you are fulfilled and abundant in every way – or you are being used by a past you no longer wish to repeat. In most cases, this past vibration is nothing but a shell, a ghost. It's like an outdated webpage that has never been removed from the Internet but can still be accessed with the right search terms. These memories, feelings, thoughts and states of being can be triggered, and will continue to be triggered, as we work to change our point of attraction. If it empowers you to think of it in these terms, you could view coming into contact with your previous point of attraction as a kind of "test" from the universe. Regardless of what choices you have made in the past, you are now being given a brand new opportunity to choose the vibration you want to live in.

From my own experience, I can tell you that these choice points usually come along when you least expect them; when things are going well and you feel like you're well on your way; when you've opened up a space within you to allow into being the future you desire...and then bam! Into this space all manner of things are attracted – a text from the former "empty calorie" boyfriend; a tempting offer to stay at the job you're in even though it drains your spirit; maybe even the recollection of a recent loss or some ancient, ancient shame. The saying "nature abhors a vacuum" speaks directly to this phenomenon. The more space you clear out inside, the more attractive you become to the entire spectrum of possibilities available to you. However, unlike in times past, now you are attracting deliberately because you have decided the vibration that constitutes your *it* and your *all*. You now have the opportunity to align with, embrace, and amplify every single instance of that new frequency that manifests in your life – whether it comes in the form of a new friend, an intriguing business opportunity, a sign of serendipity, or even a song on the radio – and to gently thank and then release everything that falls outside of your now-selected frequency. Those lower, slower vibrations will still catch your eye, I assure you. And there will be an emotional intensity to them that may be difficult to ignore. My advice? Don't ignore them. Allow them in. The thoughts, feelings and beliefs that once constituted your dominant state of being and point of attraction are like old friends that you have simply outgrown. There is no animosity; no need to hold a grudge. When you bump into these frequencies (no doubt because you're up to something that flies in the face of them), simply acknowledge them, allow yourself to feel what it's like to revisit them, and then shift your focus to what you want NOW.

The key is to breathe deeply, and to offer yourself compassion for once having been a match to that vibration, for however long you were; to acknowledge and appreciate the fact that there was a time when it served you, and that now, it no longer does. Most of all, to extend as generous an amount of gratitude to yourself as you possibly can for the awareness you now have. There was a time when you simply reacted to that vibration, making it part of your own. Now, you have a choice. As you learn to embrace rather than suppress uncomfortable feelings, to allow them rather than resist them, you literally reprogram your nervous system and alter the way you respond to life – and the way life responds to you.

— • —

PLAY SHEET FOR CHAPTER 4: Opening to Receive – Resetting Your "Allowing" Meter

Call to mind any area of your life where you are in a state of resistance – some place where you have a chronic complaint or where your viewpoint is one of "It shouldn't be like this." Reflecting on the details of this situation as it exists in this moment, see if you can allow yourself to accept it exactly as it is. Remember that accepting a situation does not mean that you approve of it, or that you don't want it to change. It simply means accepting what is at this moment. Give yourself permission to think and feel about it the way that you do, without trying to minimize your feelings or pretend to feel any differently.

As you pay closer attention to the way you feel about this situation, allow yourself to receive whatever information your emotions are trying to convey to you. What is the message your feelings are giving you about you?

Allow yourself to feel the intensity of your emotions fully and completely, without describing or labeling them. Simply be with them with all of your attention, and feel the power of their vibration. As you grant your feelings permission to exist – and as you embrace them rather than resist them – notice that they begin to dissipate and release.

From this new level of awareness, allow yourself to connect with what you really do want to experience in this area of your life. How do you want to feel in relation to this situation? What is one action you could take – be it an inner action or an outer action – to change your set point in relation to this subject or aspect of your life and allow in more of what you are wanting?

CHAPTER **5:**
The Manifestation Equation

I hope that by now you're getting the idea that becoming magnetic to your *it* and your *all* is a process of calling forth into physical form that which already exists as an energetic possibility. This is not a linear or sequential phenomenon, but a holographic one that takes place simultaneously within your mind, heart and solar plexus. Yes, it begins as a mental image of the specific and tangible results you desire to create, but far more important than the clarity of this vision is your ability to connect to the energy of it as already being fulfilled, and to allow this frequency to flow in and through every cell of your being. To the extent that you are connected to the energetic essence of your desire, you empower this energy to guide and direct you in ways you could not have possibly orchestrated or predicted. There are no wrong turns or dead ends, just endless variations and paths leading to your desired destination. Your only job is to align yourself with a few fundamental principles that govern the process of manifestation... they will do the rest.

What many people don't yet understand about working with the universal laws of deliberate creation is that these principles operate not in isolation, but in unison with one another. Clarity, intention, and action represent the external, masculine side of manifestation. Alignment, detachment, and allowing represent the internal, feminine side. When internal clarity is met with non-resistance, the masculine energy of intending is joined with the feminine energy of allowing, setting into motion the alchemical process that all creation is predicated upon – whether it's the creation of a child, the erecting of a temple or the birth of a galaxy. When you then add physical action into this equation, you summon the power to manifest anything you desire. Whether you experience this creative process as spontaneous and easy or as slow and difficult depends on how much of a balance you are able to strike between these inner and outer forces.

The Manifestation Equation

There are three main factors that determine how quickly and effortlessly our intentions are made manifest, and when we apply this formula in a proportion that is appropriate to each unique situation, we easily magnetize into our lives the outcomes we desire. This formula is as follows:

Clarity **+** *Alignment* **+** *Action* **=** *Manifestation*

Having mental clarity about what it is we want while at the same time maintaining a feeling state of allowing and non-resistance will always draw it towards us. It is the combination of feeling good, excited and content with what is, while at the same time being clear about what more we want, that opens the door for more to come into our lives. Intending and allowing are equally important in the manifestation equation, but every situation calls for a different degree of each. The bigger our goal and the clearer our intention, the more we need to allow.

The bigger our goal and the clearer our intention,
the more we need to allow.

When unobstructed by resistance, our body-mind system functions like a well-tuned orchestra – and designing a life in which you have it all is a lot like creating a beautiful piece of music: Desire is the baseline that drives the music forward at a particular rate and rhythm. Clarity about the exact nature of what you want builds intensity and distinguishes the unique vibration of your desire, in the same way that adding a saxophone to a song can make that piece of music distinctly sultry, funky, relaxing or even majestic. Allowing acts like the soft strumming of a guitar, or vocals that complement each chord, melding what were once separate and disparate notes into harmonic resonance. All of these elements function in concert with one another and when one is out of balance, the areas of our lives where we long to experience beautiful "music," instead become filled with chaos and discord.

Too much clarity of desire, when coupled with not enough allowing, creates too sharp of a pitch, and like nails on a chalkboard, your experience will be one of irritation, annoyance, frustration or even anger. On the other hand, if there is too much allowing and not enough clarity, the resonance of the vibration you are sending out becomes muffled and ineffectual. Emotionally you may feel bored, aimless, lethargic, resigned or depressed, and the results you are seeking will most likely come slowly if they come at all. It's also quite possible to be in a state of allowing and feel good; after all, one of the primary benefits of the Law of Allowing is that it brings us to a state of relaxation, surrender, and peace. But when allowing is not balanced by clarity of desire, we lack the creative drive that is needed to manifest our intentions. I've known a lot of people who are very good at allowing and who have practiced the art of releasing resistance when some aspect of their lives is not unfolding as they would like. Yet, very often these same people are not very practiced in the art of deliberately creating the circumstances of their lives. Creation is equal parts intending and allowing. Manifesting your *it* and *all* with the greatest amount of ease is simply a matter of striking the right balance between the two.

Plugging this into the formula of the Manifestation Equation means that you 1) **clarify** the outcome you want to create – not just in a material, tangible sense, but in how you want to feel in the having of it; 2) connect with your emotions to make sure that the frequency you are offering is **aligned** with that outcome; and 3) determine whether the situation at hand will best be served by taking outer **action,** or by focusing on aligning your internal energy instead. By aligning yourself energetically with the internal feeling state you want to experience as a result of your external creation, you call into being the 96 percent of you that exists as pure potential energy and allow it to infuse every action you take.

Inner Action vs. Outer Action

Years ago, Jack Canfield, one of my earliest mentors, shared with me a principle that has since been cited by numerous other metaphysical teachers and tested by quantum physicists: One hour of "inner" work – and by this he was referring to intending, visualizing, aligning and allowing – is worth seven hours of "outer" work. Now, doing "inner" work does not necessarily mean sitting in meditation for hours each day. What it does mean is that before we take any outer action, we first take a moment to clarify the intention behind that action. Said another way, we deliberately decide how we want to *feel,* and get into that state of *being* before we *do* anything. A few minutes of aligning your energy with the outcome you want to create is far more powerful than hours and hours of action taken without this connection. It's like the difference between using an electronic device that is running on battery power versus one that is plugged in and being fully charged by a live electrical current. Action that is infused with energy and intention produces results that are astonishing compared to what can be accomplished with action alone.

Recently, I was being interviewed by a woman who was writing an article on women who are entrepreneurs. She asked me to describe a typical day in my life, and so I started listing off the top of my head the number of things that I manage and accomplish on any given day: I am a mother to my two boys, I told her – four and five at the time of this writing – whom I care for, read to, play with and home-school. I maintain a conscious and passionate relationship with my husband, Frederic. I facilitate 25 coaching programs each year, in which I teach people the principles of deliberate manifestation and how to create the results they desire in relation to their bodies, their finances, their relationships, and every other aspect of their lives. Every month, I tape several episodes of *Quantum Success* – the show I created which airs on the YouTube channel. To date, I have trained a total of 1,500 Law of Attraction coaches worldwide, and facilitate an intensive coaching program for at least 50 new coaches each year. To support all of these programs, I travel to do media appearances, write books, blogs, magazine articles and e-zines, and conduct introductory seminars a few times a month to give people who are new to my work a feel for what I do.

In addition to managing a growing career and a multi-million dollar business, I maintain close relationships with a large extended family, both on Frederic's side in Montreal, where we live eight months out of the year, and with my family in Arizona, where we travel each year to spend our winters. Of course, as a woman in my early 40s, taking good care of my body is a high priority. I work out five days a week, get a massage every Saturday, and treat myself to a spa day, a reflexology treatment, a facial, or a trip to the acupuncturist once a month. Our family takes several vacations each year, and Frederic and I also make sure that we get away to spend quality time alone on a regular basis (Date Night, baby! ☺).

As I was answering this interviewer's question, the look that slowly crept across her face was priceless. "I'm exhausted just listening to your daily schedule," she said with a sigh. This struck me as ironic, because I'm enlivened by it. I had to smile, because her response was such a perfect confirmation that every woman has a different definition of having it all. Everything I give my energy to each day is an integral part of my *it* and my *all,* and every bit of it is a source of inspiration and personal fulfillment. The "secret" behind my ability to accomplish so much in so many different aspects of my life, I explained, is that I make it a priority to first bring my internal energy into alignment with the essence of my desire *before* I take any external action. So when I'm with my kids, for example, my vibration is aligned with my intent that our relationship be harmonious, evolving, and fun. When I'm doing something that nurtures my body, I begin by connecting with my intention to fill myself with whatever vibration I want to experience at that moment – vitality, stamina, sexuality, relaxation, increased immunity, or whatever else will best serve me. When I'm working on a project or with students in a coaching program, the frequency that I offer is one of excitement and joyful anticipation, because I know that the best possible outcome for all concerned is now in the process of unfolding.

Even if you devote just one minute out of each hour to making sure your actions are aligned with your intent, the cumulative effect of this over time is staggering – and the results you produce will be far more effective. This point was underscored in a recent conversation I had with Dr. Sue Mortor, who is known for her pioneering and truly mind-blowing work in bridging science and human potential. Like me, Sue said that she accomplishes at least four times more in her life today than she did 10 years ago, and with a greater degree of internal ease and joy, because, as she described it, she has learned "to access a deep place within my own system where there is complete alignment and infinite capacity." The place Sue is referring to is that unseen reservoir known as intention. If you've ever heard accounts about human beings doing extraordinary and "impossible" things – like lifting a car to save a child or physically carrying someone to safety whose body weighs two times their size – then you are already familiar with the power of intention. What most of us don't realize is that while times of great necessity (and great inspiration) draw this power to us naturally, we also have the ability to summon intention on purpose.

> *"There is a deep place within your system*
> *where there is complete alignment and infinite capacity."*

I was working as a pharmaceutical sales rep when I was first introduced to the practice of combining inner intention with taking external action, and my job afforded me the perfect opportunity to field test this principle and find out how effective it really was. I had already noticed that anytime I brought the "inner" or energetic aspect into my work by deliberately offering a vibration that matches what I wanted to create, my success skyrocketed. So, I conducted a little experiment: Rather than making a certain number of sales calls each day and going out on appointments, all I did was meditate, visualize, intend, and allow. Not surprisingly, my sales numbers – which had been the highest in the district – fell to among the lowest. The following month, I combined both the physical action of going out and making sales calls with the inner action of visualizing and feeling the success I wanted to create, and my numbers easily went right back up to the top. It's the combination of the two that is so powerful.

Some Law of Attraction experts I've met assert that creating internal alignment is more important than taking external action. My belief is that they are equally important. There is no magic pill; anything that we want to create requires us to put our energy into it. My friend, Bill Harris, renowned in the field of personal development and I were talking about this recently, and he made what I thought was a really good point. "The Law of Attraction has become associated with this idea that you don't have to do anything," he said. "Some folks are operating inside this misconception that you just need to identify what you want, place a picture of it on an altar, and bam, a new bicycle will appear on your porch." Some degree of action is always required to bring about the fulfillment of any goal, but *inspired action* – which is the act of being energetically aligned with how we will feel once our goal is attained – is exponentially more powerful than action taken alone.

Action without alignment can be exhausting (think dog chasing its tail, or hamster in a wheel), but action that is fueled by internal alignment has a momentum behind it that literally magnetizes miracles into our lives. As you learn to master the art of shifting your own energy field and modulating the amount of clarity, alignment and action you apply to each important area of your life, you will engineer manifestations so brilliant and so perfect that they surprise even you. This was certainly the case when I manifested my soul-mate and husband, Frederic.

Toward the end of my eight-year relationship with my former husband, I became acutely aware of the qualities in him that were no longer a match to the person I had become. Out of experiencing the contrast of what I did *not* want from an intimate relationship came greater clarity about what I *did*. Using a process I had learned from Law of Attraction coach Michael Losier, I wrote down all the qualities that I didn't enjoy about my ex, and used this list to identify the qualities that I did find attractive. As I gained more clarity about the type of relationship I wanted, I identified *companionship, connection* and *love* as the primary feelings that I wanted to experience in a relationship, and allowed myself to imagine and connect with the essence of how it would feel to be with a man like this. Once I had connected to this feeling essence, I then did a series of meditations in which I imagined sending out a clear intention to connect with this man soul-to-soul – a process which I now teach as part of my 4-week *Attracting Your Ideal Partner* program, which has helped hundreds of people find their ideal partners. Anytime my vibration in relation to manifesting the love of my life was attuned to a lower-level emotion such as loneliness, sadness or self-doubt, I would use these feelings as a reminder of my *it* and *all* desire to experience connection, companionship and love, knowing that I first needed to generate these feelings within myself before I could ever receive them from another person. Whenever I felt sad that I didn't have anyone to go to dinner with on a Saturday night, I would take myself out to a nice dinner where I would meet new friends to connect with, or I would take some other action to create the experience of love and companionship – not only with others but with myself.

My life during this time happened to be in an absolute state of flux. I was in the middle of a divorce and had just made the decision to move across the country to take a new position in my company. Everything was new and unknown. The key to keeping my intention clear and my vibration high was a new practice I had committed to: I started listening to and acting on the impulses that arose from within me. I had suppressed most of these impulses when I was married, probably because I sensed that following them would lead me to continued growth and would therefore create even more distance between my ex and me. Now that I had released that relationship, I was free to let myself be guided from within.

One such impulse came one night as I was literally packing boxes in preparation for my upcoming move to Philadelphia. It occurred like a flash of remembrance: Clear as day, a voice inside said, "Go online and register for the next *Warrior* conference." I complied, and signed up for the next conference, which happened to be scheduled three months from then (this was April; the event would take place in August), in Ellenville, New York.

Those three months flew by, as I was busy getting settled into my new life in Philadelphia. The day I drove from Pennsylvania to New York for the conference, I felt so joyful and happy. Because I was already so connected to myself, I felt completely full inside. I also had the sense that something big was about to happen for me personally as a result of attending, but I had no idea what it would be. Then, at one point as I was driving, I heard another voice inside my head say, "You're going to meet him at the conference." The message came through so loud and clear that I began to get really excited, but then I quickly reminded myself that I was going to the conference for me and not to meet a man.

The conference began on a Sunday night, and I was immediately drawn to an extremely attractive man who was sitting a few rows in front of me. My first thought was, "Wow. He is *hot.*" I also noticed that he was talking with a very pretty, slender Asian woman who had long, straight dark hair. They appeared to be a couple. Even though I had had premonitions of meeting my soulmate during this particular weekend, I had no hopes of anything happening with this man. That same night, we were all asked to stand and introduce ourselves, and when the gorgeous guy stood up and said his name, "Frederic," he did it with such strength and power. I remember thinking, "That's the kind of man I want to be with – powerful and strong." Again, I quickly let the thought go.

The next day was the first official day of the retreat. I had been hanging out with two guys, Heath and Kevin, who were local to the area and really fun. As I drove with them and two other participants to the first event, we talked about our shared commitment to working out and staying in shape. As it turned out, the first event would involve a hike. The instructors asked us to rate ourselves as a beginner, intermediate or advanced hiker, and to get in the corresponding line. I stood in the intermediate line and Heath and Kevin stood in the advanced. The two of them began teasing me for choosing the intermediate hike, saying that someone with my level of fitness should be with them in the advanced line – so I took the challenge.

As soon as I changed lines, our instructor appeared and asked us to pair up and find a partner. The next thing I know, Frederic was standing directly in front of me and asked, "Would you like to be my partner?" I managed to squeak out a casual "Sure," but in my head, I was thinking "Oh hell yes!"

Our "challenge" was to complete a very intense hike up a mountain, during which we were asked to remain completely silent. These instructions did not work well for me, given that I am not exactly the quiet type. Here I was with the hot guy in the group, and he wanted to talk – so we did. We kept getting chastised by the instructors: "Essential Silence!" they would yell, and for a moment we would comply, only to resume the conversation as soon as watchful eyes were no longer on us. I felt a connection with this man that was unexplainable; it was bigger than me. With him, I felt like I was home.

As we walked and talked, Frederic made it VERY clear that the woman who had accompanied him to the conference was his "business partner." *Hmm*, I thought. The door I thought was closed was actually wide open. When we joined back up with the larger group, Frederic started talking to a man named Bill, also from Montreal, about the fact that Bill had a house for sale and Frederic was in the market to buy. As I listened to them talk about the selling price and other details about Bill's house, I suddenly heard a voice inside my head say, *"No. Wait for me."* I was shocked. After all, I'd only known this man for an hour. Later that day, we did a group activity where we went from person to person, saying a mantra. When I got to Frederic, he said, "Now I am with the right partner." My heart jumped, and I felt total butterflies. At the end of the day, as I was walking through the hall of the hotel on my way back to my room, I saw Frederic walking towards me. "There's the Goddess," he said as we passed each other. I managed to muster a "hi" in return. In reality, I felt like I was about to pass out because I was so attracted to and moved by him. In addition to feeling connected to him, I felt *seen* by him.

During these first few days of the conference, I was receiving a lot of attention from a couple of other men at the event, but I felt no attraction toward them. I was crystal clear about the qualities that I wanted in a partner, and was also quite content to be with myself rather than settle for a man who was not a match to my vision. The other men at the retreat didn't even come close.

Each morning of the conference began with everyone doing yoga and dancing. On one particular morning, the women were asked to move to one side of the room and the men to the other. Then, we were to dance toward the center and over to the other side of the room. Perfectly orchestrated by the Law of Attraction itself, Frederic and I ended up right in front of each other. The moment we were in each other's energy fields, we started to dance together, and we got so into harmonizing with the music and with one another that when I finally looked up from this vortex of energy that we had generated between us, all the women were already on their side of the room and the men were on the other. Frederic and I were alone in the middle of the room, and all eyes were on us. Frederic was celebrated when he got back to the men's side and the women kept asking me, "How did you do that?"

After that, people were coming up to us and asking us how long we had been together. Several couples assumed that we were already married. Still others were trying to play matchmaker, giving us sales pitches as to why we should be together because of the undeniable chemistry between us. The guys that were interested in me tried extra hard to get my attention after seeing Frederic and me dancing together, but I was not the least bit interested in them.

The next day, as we walked to our next event – a sweat lodge – we were asked to pair up and hold hands. Frederic and I immediately sought each other out, and the minute he touched my hand, something happened to me. I felt an amazing connection and blending with him. The sweat lodge was an emotional and very spiritual experience for me. I remember looking at Frederic in the lodge and thinking, "I am in love with this man. I have never even kissed him, and I am in love with him." It was one of those moments in my life that I will never forget. Every time I think about it, I am drawn right back to that time, and I can feel the experience of it all over again. He asked if I would take a walk with him after the seminar ended that night. The hours of the seminar were crazy: yoga started at 6 a.m. and the last event of the day didn't end until 11 p.m. or 12 a.m. We were only getting a few hours of sleep, but I didn't care – the idea of spending time with him alone sounded amazing.

After the event that night, we walked around the old hotel, built sometime in the 50s, and into a wooded area with lots of trees and pathways. We found a big rock to sit on and talk together. As we were talking, I could feel him shaking, and the butterflies in my stomach, too. We got close enough to feel each other's breath – and then he kissed me. Without going into too much detail, it was the most romantic moment of my entire life. We stayed up kissing and talking until about 2 a.m. that morning, and thanks to the adrenaline of being in love, waking up at 5:30 a.m. was no big deal. In fact, I would have stayed up all night if it meant getting to see him again.

I saw him the next morning at yoga, and I couldn't wait to talk with him. I couldn't wait to touch him. I couldn't wait to kiss him. We ended up getting placed in different groups, so I didn't see him much that day. But that night, I picked him to catch me after I did a fire walk, which was the final event of the conference. Everyone was leaving the next day. The conference was over.

After the fire walk celebration, we went on another walk. This time we walked to my car and climbed into the backseat of my convertible Audi like two high school kids. Frederic is five foot eleven and there was not much room back there, but we didn't care. We were so completely into one another. As we said goodbye that night I told him, "My roommate is leaving tomorrow at 8 a.m." To this, Frederic replied, "I'll be there at 8:01!"

The next morning, I watched happily as my roommate packed up and left the room, and at about 8:15, I heard a knock at my door. I opened it up. Frederic said, "Hi," and those were the last words that were spoken. There were no thoughts, no conditions, no considerations or "what ifs." We both just surrendered to the energy of that moment – the energy that we had both intended and summoned. The next thing I knew we were laying together on my single bed, kissing and making love. It was one of the most amazing and passionate experiences of my life.

After it was all over, I had no idea when or where or even if I would see him again. I lived in Pennsylvania and he lived in Montreal. When we finally said goodbye and he left the room, I just fell to the floor and started to cry. I didn't feel sad because he lived in a different country. I didn't feel worried about if or when I was going to see him again. I wasn't thinking about how or if things would work out. I was in love and yet so detached. I just got on my knees and said, "Thank you. Thank you. Thank you. I don't know what this will lead to or where it will go. I am just happy that I experienced this. Thank you."

As I was pulling out of the hotel parking lot and about to drive away, Frederic walked in front of my car and planted the biggest kiss on my lips. The same song was playing on the radio that had been playing the night before when we were in the back of my car. The lyrics were "Whenever you need me, I will be there for you." I have never been able to find that song, or who sang it, and I have never heard it again since. But it was perfect for the moment. As the song was playing on the radio, he showed up and kissed me. Amazing.

On the drive back to Pennsylvania from New York, Frederic called me, using a cute excuse about how his roommate had something stolen from the hotel room and was I missing anything? We talked on the phone for a bit as I drove. We talked every day since that day, and saw each other every two weeks until I moved to Montreal a few months later. The man that I had been envisioning, and the intimate relationship I desired, had manifested in my life. I could not have orchestrated this if I tried. Two months before we met, I was a woman living in California and he was a man living in Montreal, Canada. To be honest, I didn't even know there was a Montreal, Canada!

The universe holds a bird's eye view of our lives and is more than capable of managing all the pieces of the puzzle that make up our ideal and perfect whole. When we surrender our need to figure out how, who, what, when and where it will happen, and place our attention instead on simply aligning ourselves in heart and mind to the essence of our desire, the universe makes it happen for us. There is no pushing, shoving, manipulating, planning, or any of the other strategies that we've been taught to use to go after what we want. By surrendering the illusion that we are in control and simply allowing things to unfold, we summon the power of the Law of Detachment, which states that the fastest way to manifest any outcome is to relinquish our attachment to it. When you know that there are truly an infinite number of ways that your *it* and *all* can come into your life, you can allow things to unfold in their own timing.

I share the story about how I met Frederic because, for me, it is one of the most powerful cases in point of the role that all the universal laws play in the manifestation of a desire. It's not merely a matter of intending, or of allowing. As I often say, it's not *either/or;* it's *both/and.* It's not like there is a specific stage in each manifestation where one law is indicated above any other. It truly is a creation that we participate in moment by moment, that is both registered by and orchestrated by our own energy field. I think this is why I like the parallel between manifesting a desire and making music. It really is a dance between inner and outer, between asserting and yielding, intending and allowing. We can always tell by how we feel in the creating of it what kind of experience we are in the process of manifesting. We can tell by tuning in to ourselves to discover the energy that is driving our behaviors, and by asking ourselves – as Marianne Williamson shared during a recent conversation – "Am I acting from my healed place or from my wounded place? Which aspect of my being am I bringing forward in this moment?"

"Am I acting from my healed place or from my wounded place? Which aspect of my being am I bringing forward in this moment?"

If you're clear about what you desire but are bumping up against what Marianne referred to as the "wounded place" within you, or you are encountering any other form of resistant thoughts or feelings, what is called for in that moment is a backing off of desire and an increase in allowance. Take a break from whatever you are doing. Practice appreciation for the present moment as it is. Break down whatever it is you are working toward into smaller "bites." Give yourself compassion. Allowing makes healing available. Once we drop our resistance, we can then be informed by our emotions. We can shift old or non-serving beliefs, and replace the energy of the old belief with the energy of a new, more empowering belief.

On the other hand, when in the creative process there is too much allowing and not enough clarity, know that all that is needed is to strengthen your desire and refocus upon your intended outcome. Ask yourself, "What do I want to feel in this situation, and why?" Clarify within yourself the frequency and feeling essence you want to experience. Do you want to feel passion? Reassurance? Love? Clarity of desire produces a quickening and allows us to move toward our intended outcome with greater focus.

The great news about creating your *it* and your *all* is that, like orchestrating a piece of music, you get to make it as big and bold as you want it. If what you're creating feels too chaotic, you can tone it down. If it gets too boring, you can add in whatever notes you like. This is the fine-tuning element of being a deliberate creator. Now that you understand the main principles involved in any manifestation, you can play with each of the components so that you can offer the precise frequency that is called for in every situation.

— ● —

CHAPTER 5 PLAY SHEET:
The Manifestation Equation

Notice a particular area in your life where you are experiencing either impatience or discouragement in relation to the fulfillment of a goal or desire that you hold dear, and challenge yourself to remember that these emotional states are simply symptoms of an imbalance in the Manifestation Equation. See if you can identify – based on the way you feel – whether the situation would best be served by generating more *clarity* or more *allowing*.

If more clarity is called for, revisit your vision of having it all and the way you desire this part of your life to look and feel. What do you want and why do you want it? What impact will the creation of it have on you physically, emotionally, mentally and spiritually? Why is this so important to you, and what is the next logical action you can take toward creating it?

If more allowing is needed in relation to this situation, deliberately look for everything in your life that works and that you appreciate. Acknowledge and celebrate yourself for all the energy you have put forth to transform this area, and remind yourself that this energy is a living vibration that is even now gathering towards it what you have declared that you want. Your only job now is to breathe and receive.

CHAPTER **6:**
Calling Forth the Essence of Your Desire

Behind every desire – big or small, material or intangible, superficial or deep – is a longing to experience a certain feeling. Examine the desires that have been evoked within you as you are now thinking deeply about your definition of having it all – whether it's to meet your soulmate, transform your body, experience more fulfillment in your career, or make more money – and you will discover that the underlying reason you want any of these things is because you believe having them will make you *feel* a certain way. To uncover the inner feelings driving your desire for external things, you need only ask yourself one question: *Why do I want it?* If you desire more money, for example, it's probably not because you like the way it looks or enjoy the feeling of paper between your fingers. You want it because you are longing to experience a deep, essential feeling that you believe the money will bring. It might be a feeling of worthiness, of empowerment, of self-love, of freedom...This feeling is the essence of your desire. No matter what you want to create in the outer world, what you are really seeking is the feeling of this internal "essence." Learning to connect with and vibrate in energetic resonance with the essence of what you want to manifest, *while it exists in its unmanifested form,* is the key to attracting it into your life. When you tap into the essence of your desire, you bridge the gap – sometimes slowly and sometimes unbelievably quickly – between where you are and where you want to be. Let me give you an example from my own life.

Fifteen years ago, after I was asked to resign from my job in pharmaceutical sales – an industry I had worked in for nearly seven years – I felt utterly and completely lost. Not only because I had no idea how I would make a living, but also on a more basic level, I felt lost because I had always identified myself as someone who worked, and without a job, I had lost that sense of identity. At that time, I literally didn't know who I was. I felt aimless, without purpose, without passion, and without a clue as to what actions I could take to get back on track. I had just completed a course called Awakening Your Light Body, which is about learning how to connect with and direct the body's vibrational energy centers. The idea occurred to me to practice using what I had learned in that course to awaken within the energy centers of my body the feeling essence of purpose and passion. I had no idea what my life would look like if I felt passionate and on purpose; I just kept connecting with the essence of these feelings – not as a concept in my mind but as an energy that I called forth and felt in my body.

It was during one of these meditations that I saw the title to a book – *Perfect Pictures*. That same night, and for seven nights in a row thereafter, I woke up at 1:05 a.m. with all the information for my first book rushing like a river into my head. I couldn't write fast enough to keep up with it. Calling forth the feeling essence of purpose and passion is literally what set me on the path to finding the work that I love; the publishing of that first book launched my career as an author and a coach. A huge part of my *it* and my *all* is having the honor to share what I know to be my true gifts through my books, teleclasses and coaching programs. Although I didn't have the language at that time to describe the process as clearly as I do today, evoking the internal, feeling essence of any external desire continues to be one of the most powerful ways I know to manifest it into our lives.

Of course, most of us learned a completely opposite approach to going after the things we want. If this approach were written as a formula, it would look something like this: "When I *achieve* X, then I will *feel* Y." Each of us solves for Y according to our own value systems. Some of us believe the happiness we seek will come to us when we finally find the right man, or when we have a child, or when we get that big promotion. We may think it will be ours when we reach our ideal body weight or clothing size, or move into the house of our dreams. To some extent, all of us have been conditioned in the mindset that attaining some external condition or object will bring us internal fulfillment. When we follow this outside-in path to happiness, we may achieve some degree of success, but it takes a lot of effort, often leaving us cranky and exhausted – not exactly how we'd hoped we would feel once we accomplished that particular goal.

I, for one, was definitely raised with the belief that if I wanted to be successful, I needed to work hard and go after what I wanted with full force. This is the way I operated, with some measure of success, for the first decade of my adult life. What I know now is that while this masculine outside-in approach is part of the formula for manifesting our desires – because after all, creation in the physical world must involve some action – evoking the "inside-out," feminine aspect of creation yields better results, in shorter time, and in a way that is infinitely more rewarding.

To take the outside-in approach to having it all is to continually chase the outer conditions (the job, the house, the relationship, etc.) that we believe will make us feel better inside. It's rooted in the premise that we are incomplete as we are and that our happiness depends on sources outside of ourselves. Watch an episode of *The Bachelor* and you'll see a perfect example of this. Here are these bright, beautiful, educated women who have been hypnotized to believe that only when they find their Prince Charming will they be complete. Each week another lovely young woman bursts out in tears of desperation, sobbing that she hasn't yet found "The One" and sure that when she does, he will be the answer to all her woes. The inside-out approach represents a 180-degree turnaround from this way of thinking. Instead of going after the external result, hoping it will bring us the internal feeling we're seeking, we first generate within us the feeling we desire, and from that feeling state we magnetize our desire. It's a shift in mindset from "When I get the job, I will feel confident," to "When I align myself with the feeling of confidence, I will attract the job."

Eight years ago, when I realized that the next piece of creating my *it* and *all* was to find my soulmate and start a family, I used this inside-out approach of connecting with the essence of my desire in order to attract him. After making a list of all the qualities that I wanted in a partner, I allowed myself to vividly imagine all the things we would enjoy doing together. I then identified the bottom-line feeling that I wanted to experience in an intimate relationship. The essence I was seeking was one of *connection*.

For the next couple of months, I focused on connecting – with others, yes, but more importantly with myself. After my daily meditations, I would check in with myself and ask questions like, "How are you feeling? What do you feel like doing today? What would make you feel really connected?" Then I would listen to the answers and follow through on what I heard. Learning to become a better friend to myself guided me step-by-step from a vibration of isolation to one of connection. The more connected I felt, the more magnetic I became. And because I had practiced aligning my energy with the feeling of being connected, I was able to allow myself to make an incredibly deep connection with Frederic in a very short period of time. This was key, given that we lived in different countries and met at a weekend leadership retreat. We didn't have time to mess around!

If this inside-out approach to manifesting were written as a formula, it would look like this: "When I *feel* Y (essence feeling), I will be an energetic match to X (what I want to create) and from that feeling, I will magnetize it to me." When we align ourselves – our thoughts, emotions, images and beliefs – with the essence of our desire, we draw it to us on the current of our vibration, invisibly and yet powerfully magnetizing it into our lives.

Achieving the essence of your desire feeds you, inspires you, and fulfills you...not the day when you finally meet the right man; not the day when you have the money in the bank; but *right now,* in this very moment. Connecting to the essence is the fastest possible way to get into energetic alignment with your *it* and your *all,* because nothing in your outer world has to change in order for you to experience the feeling you are seeking. Nothing is missing. There is nothing to chase. Those essence qualities are immediately available to you and in infinite supply because they exist at your very core. You are not seeking love; you *are* love. You don't have to earn abundance; abundance is your birthright. When I interviewed John Burgos, the founder and host of the transformational *Beyond the Ordinary* tele-summit, he described so beautifully both how it feels to be energetically aligned with the essence of our desire, and how to call that essence forward into our lives: "When you really allow yourself to connect with how that potential outcome is going to feel, you are actually projecting forward into that specific future and bringing gratitude and success into your now," he said. "And what's really amazing," he continued, "is that by allowing yourself to swell up with that gratitude, you open up doorways along your path. Synchronicity comes into play and people show up in your life that bring you to places that are truly unimaginable to you in the present moment." John is right. From the state of gratitude, you become magnetic to all that you want to attract into your life, and open to receive the version of your *it* and *all* that is written in the blueprint of your soul.

> *"By allowing yourself to swell up with that gratitude,
> you open up doorways along your path. Synchronicity comes
> into play and people show up in your life that bring you to places
> that are truly unimaginable to you in the present moment."*

When we strive for accomplishment and material things without first aligning ourselves with the essence of the feeling we are seeking from them, we may create results, but too often they don't bring us the inner joy we had hoped they would. My coach, Karen, explains the distinction between external manifestation and inner essence as "the difference between creating your 'vision board' life, and actually *living into* that vision in a way that feels every bit as rich and abundant as it looks." If we focus only on the outer manifestation of our *it* and *all,* all we have created is a plastic flower. It's pretty to look at, but it has no fragrance, no sweetness, no essence. To pursue external success without internal alignment is to place our happiness on an altar outside of ourselves. One dent in the sought-after new car; one turn in the market that brings down the equity of our home or investments; one forgotten birthday or anniversary, and all the joy we once derived from these things falls away, because it was rooted in something external and not within ourselves. By looking deeper than *what* we want to *why* we want it, we reconnect with the bottom-line feeling that we're really searching for. The moment we redirect our attention from desiring something external to feeling its internal essence within us, we shift our feeling state from wanting to *having,* from becoming to *being,* and from striving to *allowing*…and we change our point of attraction.

Our point of attraction – the degree to which our thoughts, beliefs and emotions are in or out of alignment with our core desires – is the most powerful resource we have in every moment of our lives. It's like a lighthouse broadcasting a signal that brings home every desire floating out there in the sea of pure potentiality – or prevents them from ever reaching the shore. Our point of attraction determines whether we generate upward momentum or downward spirals; whether we are met with open doors and green lights or detours and dead ends. When what we're attracting into our lives is not a reflection of what we really want, we alone have the power to change it, because we alone have the ability to direct our own energy. Connecting with essence is like plugging into the universal stream of energy that exists everywhere, all the time, and is accessible to every one of us. Essence is nothing but energy, and energy exists both within us and without us.

Energy is the basic component of the universe, and what's most important to understand is that it exists in both a manifested and an unmanifested form. Material things that we perceive through our five senses, such as beaches, mountains, trees, cars, houses, other people, etc. are all examples of energy in its manifested form. However, everything that we could ever possibly see, hear, touch, taste, smell – and therefore desire – also exists in this moment and in every moment, in its unmanifested form; as pure potential energy. This energy is alive; it is moldable, shapeable, and formable. The way we interact with the energy of a desire that has not yet manifested determines whether we will allow it or disallow it to manifest into our lives. When we are focused on its absence, it remains in the unseen world and out of our reach. When we align our energy field with the feeling essence of already having it, we draw it across the veil and into our experience. This works according to the Law of Sufficiency and Abundance, which states that by focusing on the presence of what is wanted – by imagining it, by looking for evidence of it, and by appreciating all the ways in which we already have it – we attract to ourselves more of the same. We cannot create abundance from a state of lack. It defies law.

What's Possible for One Is Possible for All

We know from quantum physics that the universe we live in is holographic. A hologram is like a thumbnail shot of a larger picture, which is to say that every small part contains the whole. Everything that was, is, or ever will be in the future also exists within each and every one of us. Despite what our senses tell us, we are not separate from one another. Because each of us has unlimited access to the pure potential energy that creates everything in the universe, from the highest galaxy to the tiniest particle, anything that has been experienced by one can also be experienced by another. Because our universe is holographic, and because energy never dies but only changes form, all the genius, freedom, inspiration, passion, love or joy that has ever been experienced by one is available to all who choose to tap into it. But wait, there's more…

This universe is so perfectly designed that in those areas of our lives where we find it difficult to connect with the essence of our desire – we simply can't conjure how it will feel to have, for example, a half million dollars in the bank, or a fit, beautiful, healthy body – there exist archetypes of the divine feminine that embody this essence and mirror it back to us in ways that are both universal and deeply personal.

Archetypes of feminine power are found in all spiritual traditions and throughout all periods of time. They are universal symbols of strength, of nurturance, of sensuality, of fertility, of power, of lust…of every possible essence we could ever seek or desire. They exist as the priestesses, heroines, witches and queens portrayed in fairy tales, literature and art; they exist in our present day culture as iconic female luminaries who have earned our deep admiration and respect; and they exist as Goddesses in the unseen world of legend, mythology and religion.

Goddess energy expresses itself in every possible form and in every possible flavor. Each one is a perfect manifestation of a specific energetic essence, from Christianity's Mother Mary, who symbolizes nurturance and healing; to the Hindu goddess Lakshmi, the Goddess of wealth and prosperity – both material and spiritual; or the Greek Goddess Nike who represents victory and success. Whether actual or mythological, known or unknown, dead or alive – what makes each Goddess so compelling is not just her beauty, her sphere of influence, or her particular talent. We adore them because they have tapped into a universal wellspring of feminine power and they show us what is possible – not just for one but for all. Sometimes a colleague or a member of our own peer group serves as a conduit of a particular form of Goddess energy; we see in her something that we deeply desire and are ready to bring forth within ourselves. Sometimes we recognize this energy in a celebrity, or as a particular trend in our popular culture that calls our attention. It doesn't matter what form the Goddess takes. What matters is that when we recognize the particular essence that she embodies, we allow ourselves to resonate with that essence. Goddess energy serves as a conduit in making manifest the unmanifest. Let me give you an example.

About fifteen years ago, when I was just beginning to learn about the universal laws that guide the process of effortlessly magnetizing our desires, I was unfulfilled in a lot of areas of my life. One prime area of discontent was in relation to my body. Although I have now created my ideal body (and support others in creating theirs), at that time, I was thirty pounds overweight and very much out of shape – the heaviest I had ever been. I had just started dating a guy I was really interested in and was desperate to lose the weight, but nothing I tried shaved off even a single pound.

One day while standing in the checkout line at the grocery store (where I had gone to stock up on an even more limited selection of proteins and vegetables), I noticed the beautiful actress, Salma Hayek, on the cover of a magazine. I had always admired the fact that she had the exact body that I wanted and hadn't been able to create, despite all my effort. I bought the magazine and looked at her pictures again later that evening. I began thinking about the principles I was studying at the time – and specifically the one I'm sharing with you now – that because the universe is holographic, the experiences felt by one are accessible to all. I started to imagine what it would feel like to live in a body like Salma's, and I asked to become open to receive her energy.

My body, which usually felt heavy, dense, and stiff, began to feel more fluid and open. The more I connected with the essence of this modern-day Goddess, the more this energy began to run through my body. The way I thought of myself in relation to the extra weight I was carrying started to shift. Where I had previously thought of myself as struggling to pull a heavy weight uphill, and never reaching the top, I now felt lightness and ease – the essence of freedom that is part of my very soul. In that moment, my body actually felt lighter – not because I had worked hard to burn the 3,500 calories it takes to lose a pound, but because I tapped into the quality of lightness that is a part of my very being.

I had always thought I wanted to lose weight so I would have the ability to wear cuter clothes or be more attractive to men. What I discovered from this process is that beneath all of that, what I really was seeking was the feeling of freedom. As I allowed that feeling, the essence of my desire, to become my new point of attraction, new thoughts, values, actions and beliefs became accessible that helped me to create it. I no longer focused on limiting food intake, but on making choices – in clothing, in food, in exercise – that evoked within me the feeling of being free. That essence feeling led me, gradually but steadily, toward creating the body I always wanted – and always knew I was capable of having.

Of course, there is no way of knowing whether the information and energy I accessed that night actually came from Salma Hayek – but where it comes from doesn't matter. What matters is that I allowed the energy I recognized in this particular form to become a conduit through which greater well-being could flow. She just happened to be the archetype that showed up for me at the moment I was ready to create a breakthrough in the area of my weight. As soon as she caught my eye on the cover of that magazine, I felt at my very core that she embodied the fulfillment of my desire.

The fact that I was drawn to that particular woman at that particular time in my life was not an accident. It was because I recognized within her an expression of the divine feminine; a universal, essential quality that I was longing to express within myself. Now, had I not been at least somewhat aware of the universal laws and of the fundamental choice we make to either align with or resist them, I might have allowed myself to become ensnared by lower vibration thoughts that are rooted in lack and limitation; in jealousy and envy; or in comparison and competition.

When we see a woman who has something that we desire, we can choose to justify her success as the result of luck, money, status, or a ridiculously fast metabolism. We can convince ourselves that she has something we do not. We can react with jealousy or sadness when our partners appreciate the Goddess in another woman. We can succumb to thoughts of worthlessness or vindictiveness. But vital to having it all is to understand that every time we make the choice to resist instead of allow, we hold ourselves energetically apart from the very thing we desire. We cannot oppose the divine feminine and channel her at the same time. We cannot hoard resources like ideas, attention, or the admiration of others and live in a vibration of sufficiency and abundance. We cannot reject a woman because we are threatened by her beauty or talent without also cutting ourselves off from the beautiful and talented parts of ourselves.

These tactics are the result of deep wounds that most of us have sustained in relationship with other females – perhaps a mother who may not have known how to nurture us or give us what we needed, or a sister or friend whom we perceived as betraying our trust or taking away from us something we cherished. Actively working with Goddess energy heals these wounds by creating a new relationship with the feminine, in all her forms. By honoring the Goddess in other women, we bring her to life within ourselves. This is the key to using female energy in a synergistic and supportive way that enhances and expands us rather than diminishes and disconnects us.

So the next time you encounter a woman who embodies the essence of something you desire for yourself, celebrate. She is giving you a glimpse of what is possible for you – in relation to your finances, your physical well-being, your happiness. She is showing you a place in your life where you are now ready to create the essence of what you truly want; of what will truly feed you. View her as your guide and study her, for she holds a piece of your hologram. She came into your life for one reason – to accelerate your evolution and lead you to the fulfillment of your desires. Breathe her in. Allow her. Align with her. By opening yourself to the subtle energies which influence her, she becomes a conduit for the energy you are seeking.

My very first experience of Goddess energy came through my godmother, Maryanne. At the age of two, Maryanne's own mother passed away, and yet she is the most loving, caring, nurturing woman I have ever known. I once asked her how it was that she could embody the essence of nurturing mothering energy, when she had lost her own mother at such a young age. She told me that one night when she was a young girl, she felt the presence of the Virgin Mary surround her, and that she allowed that feeling to stay with her and to infuse the way she approached love, life and the way she raised her children – including me. In her presence, I *knew* that I was love and I felt my own light. Maryanne made a dramatic difference in my life because of her pure love. She never judged my behavior; she just saw me as a perfect angel. When I would cry because I was scared, she never tried to stop me from having my feelings or make me bad or wrong in any way, she would just hold and comfort me. I have always said that Maryanne is evidence that angels walk among us. She was channeling the Virgin Mary without even knowing it, and this Goddess energy directed her life and made her a conduit of love.

Stepping into Goddess Energy

Tapping into the vibration of your chosen essence by connecting with it through someone who is already expressing it in physical form is not a process for connecting to a future self, or even to your higher self. It's a process that allows you to align yourself with the essence of what you desire as it exists right now in this moment. You can choose to access it, run it, and invite it to move in and through you. You can do this because it is energy, and *you* are energy, and energy is everywhere.

Aligning ourselves energetically with a feminine archetype that embodies the essence we desire draws this essence from the unseen world to the manifest world and into our lives. The more we align with it, the more physical and material it becomes. This is not something metaphysical; it is something that is absolutely observable and if you pay attention, you will begin to notice it. When a woman is running Goddess energy, she literally stands differently, walks differently, thinks, speaks, moves and breathes differently. She is the woman who turns heads when she walks into a room; what we've been referring to throughout this book as the woman who has that "it" factor. She is genuinely attractive, and not because she is stunningly gorgeous, but because she has tapped the inner source of her beauty. She has transcended the limitations of her own individual personality and touched upon something eternal.

The practice of transcendence is key to going beyond the comfort zone of what we've known before. We as individuals may feel incapable or unworthy of doing, being, or manifesting our *it* and our *all*, but Goddess energy knows no such limitations nor harbors any such doubts. She knows she can *do* it, because she already *is* it. When we tap into this energy and allow it to shift our way of being and relating in the world, we *become* the *it* that we're seeking; right here, right now. A perfect example of this is the artist Beyoncé, who in her private life is very quiet and down-to-earth. Because being a performer demands a "larger-than-life" personality, she taught herself early in her career to channel a presence she calls Sasha Fierce, which she describes as embodying the more sexual and aggressive side of her. When it's time to step on stage and go to work, Beyoncé steps aside and allows a more powerful aspect of herself to work through her...and mesmerizes audiences of millions all around the world.

Connecting with a universal archetype of feminine power allows us as women to transcend our own personal limitations – our shyness, our insecurities, our "poor me" stories, and our 20 extra pounds – and step directly into the energy stream that draws to us exactly what we want. We don't have to work hard for it, and a lot of times we don't even have to know where it came from. I remember once hearing a story about Maharishi Mahesh Yogi, the originator of the Transcendental Meditation movement, who called a group of his staff together one day to discuss plans for an elaborate project aimed at creating world peace. As he described his vision for this project, it became clear that a great deal of resources would be needed to accomplish it. Finally, one staff member spoke up. "This is a beautiful vision," he said. "But where is all the money going to come from?" The Maharishi is reported to have answered the question without the slightest hesitation. "From wherever it is right now," he said.

"Where is all the money going to come from?"
"From wherever it is right now."

Each of the heartfelt desires that constitute your *it* and your *all* is in the process of manifesting into your life...from wherever it is right now. It is not your responsibility to know the exact route or even the exact form it will take. It may come through doors that in this moment you don't even know exist. Trust that the universe holds a bird's eye view of your life and can orchestrate far greater outcomes than you can envision for yourself. Your only job is to embrace the essence of your desire and to allow its frequency to permeate your thoughts, feelings, ideas and actions.

When you are in energetic alignment with your *it* and your *all,* and as you allow this vibration to become imprinted in your mental and emotional body, your definition of what is and isn't possible expands and evolves. Evolution is nothing more than continually reaching past and breaking through everything that keeps us apart from expressing our full potential, and desire is the force that drives that evolution. Key to allowing those desires to take form is learning to savor the sensation of wanting what we don't yet have, in the same way we enjoy making plans for a vacation that might be a year or more away, or thinking about the delicious things we're going to order on the way to a favorite restaurant. When the excitement of the *idea itself* feeds and inspires us, we are in the perfect state to allow it into our lives.

Once we dismantle the deeply ingrained conditioning that our happiness is waiting for the fulfillment of some future vision, we discover that the real joy lies in gradually bringing ourselves into alignment with that vision. Would anything in life be as sweet or as satisfying if it weren't for the gap of time between the wanting and the having? Would waking up tomorrow morning to discover that you're already married to your soulmate be as fulfilling as meeting him, falling in love, reading the signs, and then ultimately deciding that he's The One? When you're really hungry, would it be preferable to snap your fingers and suddenly be full, or to take your time contemplating the exact perfect thing you want to eat and then savoring each bite as it takes away your hunger? Because we exist in time and space, there will always be a delay between an intention we set forth in consciousness and the manifestation of that intention in physical form. But the more you come to understand yourself not just as a physical form but as an energetic being, the more you are able to perceive that the essence of everything you desire exists, right here and right now, as pure potentiality – as energy. Remember that there are only two ways to interact with energy. You can either align with it, or you can resist it. Likewise, there are two ways that you can interact with what you have identified as your *it* and your *all:* You can focus on its presence and draw it into your experience, or you can focus on its absence and hold yourself apart from it. Each choice yields radically different results.

— ● —

PLAY SHEET FOR CHAPTER 6:
Calling Forth the Essence of Your Desire

Identify a desire that you have wanted to fulfill for quite some time. It could be a wish or a dream, such as taking an exotic trip; or maybe you want to create some ideal condition, like reaching your optimal weight. Maybe you have a specific goal in mind, such as writing a book, having a child, or completing a creative project. Whatever it is, envision clearly and exactly what it is you would like to create or accomplish.

Once you've identified *what* you want, begin to ask yourself, "*Why?*" What do you think the fulfillment of this desire will enable you to do? In what ways do you think it will change the kind of person you consider yourself to be? Most importantly, how do you believe you will *feel* having created this for yourself?

Imagine this desire as if it were already fulfilled, and connect to the bottom-line feeling or energy that you want to experience from it. Is it joy? Abundance? Freedom? Love? Whatever the essence of your desire, allow yourself to connect with it at an emotional level. Feel its essence in your heart. Feel it in your belly (your power center). Allow the vibration of this energy to permeate your entire body and radiate out through every cell of your being.

Identify a female archetype – real or mythological, known to you or unknown – who embodies the essence feeling you have just identified. What is it about her that draws your attention? Imagine aligning yourself with her in every way – allowing yourself to move like she moves; think like she thinks, and to relate to others in the way that she does. As you harmonize yourself even more with this energy, allow it to shift your vibration and inform your thoughts.

From this new energetic set point that is aligned with the essence of your desire, allow yourself to become aware of any new choices or actions you are inspired to take – and connect with the energy of your essence as you take them.

CHAPTER 7:
Transforming Contrast into Clarity –
The Secret to Having It All

The moment a desire is born within us, the moment we become aware of a longing to experience something bigger, better, or different than we are now experiencing, we draw to us and through us the energy that literally creates worlds. Desire is a force which causes three things to occur simultaneously: First, it enables us to see and feel with laser-sharp clarity precisely what it is we desire. Second, it mobilizes and begins to magnetize to us the exact resources needed to fulfill that desire. And third, it heightens our awareness of the fact that – in the present moment at least – what we desire is not yet a part of our experience. In other words, desire generates *contrast*.

Contrast is what we experience when something shows up in our outer world that is out of alignment with what we have identified within ourselves as reflecting our *it* and our *all*. Sometimes it manifests as an immediate unwanted situation: An event you've been looking forward to falls through at the last minute, or your child gets hurt and has to be rushed to the hospital. At other times, contrast shows up as an accumulation of mildly aggravating factors: hitting every red light on your way to an important meeting; encountering an exceptionally rude waitress; or just having "one of those days" where you're constantly dropping or bumping into things. Whether it shows up as something mildly irritating or majorly troubling, and whether we experience it as the absence of something wanted or the presence of something unwanted, contrast serves a very specific purpose.

It draws our attention to a discord that exists between our inner desires and our outer reality, and this discord creates a point of tension that we register in our bodies and minds as a feeling of discontent, disappointment, impatience and a lot of other emotions we typically label as "negative." But it's from this very point of tension that an intention is born, and with a clarity that can only arise from raw, unfiltered feeling, a powerful signal is transmitted instantaneously through every fiber of our being: I want something different! I want something *more!!*

Once we've allowed ourselves to identify the next evolution of our *it* and our *all,* repressing this new desire becomes almost impossible, because the very act of acknowledging that we want it begins to magnetize it into physical form. Even if we never verbalize the desire to anyone, a rush of new ideas, thoughts, impulses and possibilities begin germinating in response to it, like potent little seeds sewn in the field of our consciousness. And because we live in a universe that is governed by the Law of Polarity and was literally created from contrasting forces – black and white, empty and full, wanting and having – along with these new inspirations will inevitably come new doubts and limiting beliefs. Feelings like fear, despair, impatience or frustration are actually an invaluable part of the manifestation process. Why? Because the contrasting emotions that arise in response to what we *don't* want cause us to focus with greater clarity on exactly what it is that we *do* want; they put us in touch with just how much we want it; and they compel us to make the internal and external changes needed to bring about the results we desire. So-called "negative" emotions – like intolerance, anger, dissatisfaction and indignation – when channeled properly, actively accelerate our evolution and incite us into action. I remember years ago hearing Tony Robbins say that frustration propels more people into motion than any other emotion. That is the value of contrast.

So-called "negative" emotions – like intolerance, anger, dissatisfaction and indignation – when channeled properly, actively accelerate our evolution and incite us into action.

In the same way that necessity is the mother of all invention, adversity – or the experience of not getting what we want – is the driving force behind all change. When there is discord between our inner desire and any outer condition, that discord will eventually create a tipping point. We reach a point mentally, emotionally and energetically at which we simply "can't take it anymore," and find the motivation to make whatever adjustments are necessary to bridge the gap between what we want and what we have. Let me give you an example from my own life.

Many years ago, before I started working full time as a speaker and a coach, I worked as a pharmaceutical representative at a biotech company. After my divorce, I had a strong desire to move away from the rural part of Northern California where I'd lived when I was married. My ex had grown up in that small town and I was constantly running into his family and long-time friends, which made starting a new chapter in my life as a single woman feel difficult. I had no idea where I wanted to go; all I knew is that I no longer wanted to stay where I was.

It was during this period that I happened to see a posting announcing that my company was looking for a sales training manager to work out of our corporate office, which was located in Philadelphia. Not only was the timing perfect, but the new position offered a higher salary, and the fact that I loved teaching made it even more appealing. I interviewed for the job and got it, and literally within days of deciding it was time for a change of address, I manifested one – and even had all my moving expenses paid in the process. I was now living in Pennsylvania and was very excited about my new role within the company. And, true to what I've been sharing throughout this entire book, the moment that desire was fulfilled, a new one was born.

The contrast between my previous position working in the field as a pharmaceutical sales rep and working as a sales training manager in the corporate office was immediate, and it was stark. Instead of making my own hours and appointments, I now had a fixed 8 a.m. to 5 p.m. schedule. And whereas before I had worked pretty much independently out of my own home or car and reported to a boss who lived in another state, I now had dozens of coworkers with whom I interacted on a daily basis, and a boss whose desk was literally a few feet from my own. Yet another contrasting factor was the fact that, while I was committed to doing my absolute best in this new position, I was equally committed to continue writing about and coaching others in the application of the universal laws of manifestation that I'm sharing with you here. And even though at the time my coaching practice was not financially lucrative, it was (and still is) my life's passion, and interacting with people in a way that empowered them felt very much on track with my larger purpose.

So, to make sure I was investing my energy equally in my new job and into my new passion for teaching and coaching, I worked at my job during the day, and would then write and conduct coaching sessions with clients in the evenings and on weekends. Whenever I had enough vacation time accrued, I would take it when I was out of town at a conference, because this provided an opportunity to learn more about marketing my future business without interfering with my current job.

The man I worked for was quirky, to put it mildly, and the other sales training managers had created a special nickname for him – "Eagle" – because he made it his business to watch over every little thing we did. Early on in my new position, while I was at a conference in Chicago, I made what I would later understand to be a critical mistake, and decided to skip one of the keynote sessions during one day of the conference. Bad move. Eagle had been watching. He became extremely irate, laid into me about not attending that one lecture, and put me on his "list," where I would unfortunately remain for the remainder of the time that I worked for him.

Eagle watched over me with an especially sharp eye anytime I was training a class. The students loved me and everything that I shared with them, because it was tried-and-true information which they could put to use immediately out in the field. Since I had been one of the company's most successful sales reps to date, I had a lot of experience to draw from. The trainees were grateful for the "real life" tips and guidance I gave them, and I was also receiving consistent positive feedback from people in other departments that I was doing a great job as a trainer.

After I had just finished teaching the final class in a particular module, Eagle pulled me aside and wrote me up, stating that I had not followed the exact lesson plan. In fact, I had followed the lesson plan, but made the decision to leave out the piece that I believed was the least critical, for the simple reason that there was a lot of material to cover and we were running short on time. There was no such thing as making a mistake with this man. Despite earning rave reviews on the trainings I conducted, I was placed on an even shorter leash.

Eagle prided himself on knowing everything, which could be why he often went through my office when I wasn't there – I found out from a coworker that she had seen him doing this on several occasions. But what started as micro-management of my every action at work escalated into harassment, and eventually stalking, that went far beyond the scope of my 8-5 job: Several months after approving a request for vacation time, Eagle had gone on my website, figured out that the reason I had asked for those dates off was because I had a book signing scheduled in New York at that time, and then denied the vacation time that had already been approved.

Eagle also had a habit of giving me assignments which made no logical sense and were therefore destined to fail from the beginning. Once, he asked me to draft a sales presentation that went way beyond the indications we were allowed to publically claim for a particular drug, and to then create an algorithm based on the results that physicians had noted from prescribing the drug to patients. Even though it made no sense to me, and even though I would never use a strategy like this to sell – or to instruct others in how to sell – a medication, I did as I was told. By this time, I was all too familiar with the consequences if I failed to follow his instructions to the letter. Later, when senior managers questioned why a sales model like this had been created when the product claims were so far removed from the indications for the drug, Eagle threw me under the bus, stating that the project had been my idea from the beginning. Hopefully, you're starting to get a feel for the degree of contrast I had created in relation to my career.

No matter what I did, it was never good enough and regardless of whether I succeeded or failed, I was criticized. Eventually I spoke out to a coworker, who told me that I was not the only employee who had been targeted by this man. It turned out that several other grievances for harassment had been filed against him, and that the company had settled these grievances with the employees privately, as an incentive to drop their claims. One employee, who had filed a claim but was still working for the company in another department, encouraged me to meet with the Human Resources department and tell them about the ways I was being treated. I did, and just like before, HR opened a claim. When the HR staff interviewed the other people in my department, they discovered that Eagle was not only harassing me, but many of them as well. My frustration only grew, because for some reason this man was still permitted to work there in a management position, and day after day, I was in the position of having to interact with him.

The ironic thing is that at the same time I was experiencing this intense conflict and tension at work, my coaching practice – which was so rewarding and enjoyable – was thriving. So was my personal life. After all, it was on the heels of moving to Philadelphia to take this job that I met Frederic at that weeklong retreat. Our relationship was quickly deepening and I was becoming more determined by the day to create a business that would allow me the freedom to once again set my own hours or to move to Montreal, if I desired, to be with him.

My *it* and *all* in relation to my career at that time were crystal clear: I wanted to be my own boss and make my own hours. I did not want to answer to anyone, least of all a man who seemed to thrive on making my life a living hell. I wanted to spend more time with Frederic in Canada. Most important, I wanted the work that I did to contribute to and enhance the quality of people's lives, and I wanted to use my time and talents in a way that felt aligned with my soul's purpose, which I was getting greater clarity about all the time. If it had not been for Eagle and his incessant criticism, subterfuge, abuse and harassment, my desire to work for myself in a field that empowered and inspired me may not have gathered the traction that was needed to successfully make the jump. The intense contrast between the way I wanted to feel when I went to work and the way that I felt working for him not only drove me inward to heal the parts of me that were still a vibrational match to criticism and abuse, it also got me motivated and got me moving. If I had a supportive and nurturing boss, I may never have found the courage to quit that job and go full time with my coaching practice. Eagle – and the massive amounts of contrast he brought into my experience – is at least partially responsible for launching my career as I know it today. While I despised him at the time, I am now grateful for the role that he played.

Abusive bosses, quarreling children, a lingering cold or other physical ailment...All of these are part of life, because life *is* polarity. The important thing for us to remember is that any time something is drawn into our experience that opposes the experience we want, we are faced with a fundamental choice: We can focus on and complain about all that appears to be falling apart, or we can use that contrast to clarify exactly what we want to rebuild in its place. Regardless of our circumstances, we always have options in the way we perceive and approach them.

Nine Options

When contrast arises, meaning that something shows up that we think of as a problem or a situation or circumstance that we don't want to experience, we always have at least nine options in the way we choose to approach it. This idea was first introduced to me by Karen, who as you already know is my coach and one of my greatest teachers. She hooked her thumbs together in front of her heart with her hands facing me. Then she wiggled her fingers and said, "At every moment, each one of our fingers is pointing us to one of nine paths we can take." I later learned from Karen that placing the hands facing out toward the world while the thumbs are connected together at the heart is actually an ancient mandala that symbolizes freedom. When our hands are in this position, they take on the shape of a butterfly – reminding us that we are always free to fly in the direction of our own choosing.

As true as it is that these nine options exist, it is also true that we alone make the choice whether or not to look for them. If we stay focused only on the contrast in our lives, and not the choices that we have the power to make in response to it, we limit our ability to see options that might be right in front of us. And when we do this, of course, we end up feeling even more trapped and attracting even more contrast. Only when we are willing to start looking at our options do we start to find them. Only when we're willing to let go of our attachment to scarcity are we able to once again open up to abundance. Sarah, a woman I coached several years ago, did amazing work on this in the time we spent together. Her story offers a perfect case in point.

For the better part of her seven-year marriage, Sarah's husband treated her in a way that was disrespectful and verbally abusive, and she had grown beyond tired of the abuse. She was no longer happy in this relationship and was clear that she wanted to leave, but she also believed that she had no choice except to stay, because he was the one with all the money, and controlled the money as a means of controlling her. The contrasting experience of being in a constricting, abusive relationship gave birth to new intensions and desires within her, but believing that she was without choice in the situation kept her stuck in the contrast.

I suggested to Sarah the idea that there were at least nine options available to her, including the option of staying in the relationship, and asked her if she would be willing to look for them. As it had in my career, contrast had urged her to the point of taking action, and to her credit she jumped into this assignment with both feet. After thinking for a few minutes, things slowly began to come to mind. She said that she had a friend whom she knew would take her in until she was able to find a job and get her own apartment. She said that she could go find a job right away and start saving up to rent a place of her own. She could go live with her sister in another state, or ask her brother for a loan to cover her moving expenses. As she began thinking about all the options that were open to her, instead of thinking only about all the ways she felt trapped, ideas that she hadn't before considered suddenly came into view. Eventually, she arrived at the option that felt the best: The money she had saved from her parents' estate was in her name only, and it was hers to do with whatever she pleased. And while she had always envisioned using this money as a college fund for the children she had hoped to one day have with her husband, she now realized that she could also choose to use it to buy her own condo. It turns out, she had been holding the ticket to her own freedom all along.

Sarah's realization that she did in fact have a choice in this situation immediately filled her heart with inspiration and started her mind spinning with new possibilities. Within what was truly a remarkably short period of time, she extricated herself from a life in which she felt controlled and belittled and started creating, choice by choice, a new life about which she felt totally excited and emboldened. The seeds for this major life transformation were planted when Sarah bravely acknowledged that the contrast in her marriage had become unbearable. Those seeds took root when she became willing to seek out every possible option that was open to her – even those that were less than ideal – and to allow these options to bring her a feeling of freedom and relief. It is the feeling of freedom that makes us magnetic to our *it* and our *all*.

Whatever the contrasting experience that comes our way – whether as a relationship that is no longer nourishing us or a job that diminishes rather than fuels us – it always feels like a threat to the most essential desire that lives at the very core of each and every human being – the desire to be *free*. If we tell ourselves we have no options, we feel stuck and therefore horrible because – in the words of the non-physical guides known as Abraham – the very basis of our life is freedom. Any place in our lives where we feel that our freedom is being threatened, our perception narrows, our emotions constrict, and we become a prisoner of that situation. If in those moments we can remember – as my client did – that there are always nine options in every situation, and if we commit to start looking for them, we will start to find them. And as we do, what we will find are more things to focus on which we truly do appreciate, and – as you know – what we focus on expands. This, by the way, is the textbook definition of an "upward spiral." By acknowledging and being genuinely grateful for all the options that we have, our field of vision expands, our emotional state is uplifted, and we are better able to recognize the steps we can take to bring about the changes we desire.

Whenever contrast makes us aware of an unwanted situation that we feel powerless to change, the most important thing we can do is to remind ourselves that the one thing we always, *always* have is the power to change the way we feel about any given situation. And because we have the power to change our feelings and to consciously direct our internal responses, we also have the power to change any external outcome that we desire. When I interviewed business coach Pamela Bruner as part of my research for this book, she shared a powerful way that she reminds herself that she always has the freedom to choose, even when circumstances may appear otherwise. "Who do I want to be in this situation?" she asks herself. Depending on the circumstance, she explained, the answer to this question will vary, but the answer is never, "I want to be a victim!" It's usually along the lines of, "I want to be a person of gratitude. I want to be a person of trust. I want to be a person of power who is committed to finding solutions that are in the highest interest for me and everyone concerned." This single question cuts through contrasting experiences with laser precision, leaving us in the clarity of what we do want, instead of what we don't. This is freedom in its purest form, and it's also the path to utilizing contrast in the way it was intended: as a jumping off point toward whatever it is we wish to experience next, and to draw that experience into our lives from the inside out.

"Who do I want to be in this situation?"

You: An Evolving Masterpiece

The contrast that exists in your life at this very moment is simply the point of tension that allows you to determine what your driving intention is at each evolving moment of your life. Having it all is not like getting a diploma that hangs forever on the wall, unchanged. Because you are continually growing and expanding, you will continue to define and redefine your concept of what this means to you, at each stage and through every phase you grow through. Simply stated, the more desires we fulfill, the more desires are born within us asking to be fulfilled. The term "work in progress" is misleading in this context, because it implies a finish line. A better way to look at it, I think, is that each of us is a masterpiece that continues to become more distinct, more refined and more uniquely beautiful as it evolves. The "paint" stays forever wet and there is always more for us to create. I can tell you that I have been actively creating and re-creating my *it* and my *all* for over eighteen years, and even though I have manifested everything I have wanted up to this point in my life, I also realize that as long as my heart is beating, I will continue to generate new desires and intentions – and these will be born in me through the powerful agent of contrast. Because we live in an abundant universe, there is always more. Even if you already have an abundance of love, success, joy, freedom… there is *always* more for you to experience, for the simple reason that the universe never ends.

To be alive is to encounter contrast. It exists in every relationship, every situation, and every moment. Think about it. To allow yourself to enjoy a sumptuous meal is nothing more than setting yourself up to be hungry again. To allow yourself to love and become intimate with another human being is to open yourself to the experience of longing to be with that person again. The art of having it all lies in understanding that the experience of life is a polarity that encompasses both emptiness and fullness; the wanting as well as the having. It's not this or that, but *all* of it. When experiences arise along the journey to our *it* and our *all* that bring our awareness to the fact that we don't yet have *it,* these are simply an indication that we are not yet in complete alignment with our desire. There is inner work to do – through both sweeping strokes and gentle refinements – to craft our masterpiece in the way we've decided that we now want it to be.

Most of us, if we were given the choice, would choose to snap our fingers and make our lives an instant masterpiece. And yet if we had the power to do this, we would actually be depriving ourselves of the most valuable part of the manifestation process, which is the inner journey that unfolds as we confront, address, and adjust those beliefs, self-concepts, and patterns of thought and behavior that are no longer in alignment with who we are at our core, and who we desire to become. During a recent conversation, my friend and colleague, GP Walsh explained the role of contrast perfectly: "The uniqueness and complexity and difficulty of the obstacles we run into are caused entirely by us trying to be something we're not. The way to be satisfied is to be yourself." When you think about it, true satisfaction comes from the process of feeling our way through the obstacles that present themselves in our path – because it's by overcoming these obstacles that we gain more clarity about who we are and what we want. The real value of contrast is that it reveals the places within ourselves that are not yet vibrationally up to speed with our hearts' desires. It's a mirror, and the outer reflection changes as we create inner change.

"The way to be satisfied is to be yourself."

The most exciting part of manifestation is *not* the "getting." It's the *becoming.* It's in the process of making the adjustments to become an energetic match to our ever evolving desires that we realize that no external thing is the source of our fulfillment. We are the source of our fulfillment. The essence of all that we seek exists within us in seed form; ours to nourish and bring to life. To seek that fulfillment outside of ourselves is to become enslaved by a constant longing for the next thing and the next thing after that. Here is a great case in point:

I'll bet that you, like me, have known at least one woman who wants so badly to become pregnant because she is sure the experience will "complete" her. She tries everything available and doesn't become pregnant, until the contrast of not being able to manifest her desire forces her to find ways to "complete" herself, independent of the experience of having a baby. Because her desire didn't manifest externally, she must now evolve and expand her thinking. In the case of my friend Gretchen, the fulfillment of what she determined to be her *it* and *all* did eventually manifest – but only because she allowed it to come through an entirely different avenue than she had ever envisioned. Instead of continuing to try to get pregnant, she sought other ways to achieve the essence of her desire, and channeled her maternal, nurturing energy into developing deeper relationships within her community of friends. And – as you probably guessed – not long after she stopped fighting against contrast and started exploring other options for creating the experience of feeling "complete," she became pregnant.

All the universe is ever waiting for is for our vibration to shift from one of *wanting it all* to *already having it all*. The moment we make this internal shift, we create the space for its external counterpart to manifest in our lives. Emotionally and energetically speaking, the best possible place we can stand in order to manifest anything we want is to be satisfied with where we are in the moment, while also looking forward to all that is in the process of unfolding in the future. The experience of contentment, abundance and satisfaction is the only doorway through which more contentment, abundance and satisfaction can enter. And because these essential feelings exist and can be evoked from within us, we have the power to create the experience of abundance in any area of our lives where we are currently experiencing lack. Appreciation for who and where and how much you are right now creates the opening for more to come through. If you don't open the door, your *it* and *all* can't get in. It really is that simple.

> *The experience of contentment, abundance and satisfaction is the only doorway through which more contentment, abundance and satisfaction can enter.*

So...can you still have it all when you've been impatient with your kids and haven't been showing up as the parent you want to be? Can you still feel that you have it all when you're sick; when you've lost your voice, your ability to work out, or even the energy to get out of bed? Can you still have it all when something you've been working on in your business is not turning out the way you had hoped, or when one of your most loyal clients is now listening to one of your "competitors"? Can you still feel that you have it all when it seems everything in your life is in contrast? The answer is yes. Yes, because your inner experience is not created or determined by external things. And also yes, because you have the choice to focus on the feeling of not yet having what you want, or to conjure the feeling of your desire already being fulfilled.

Remember that we are always being called to evolve – and sometimes tragedy places the call. Clarity about what we do want arises most dramatically when we are in the presence of what we really *don't* want. Death, divorce, and all other times of transition and challenge demand us to expand beyond the self we have known and to redefine, yet again, what captures our *it* and our *all*. Contrasting experiences accelerate our evolution, and when we embrace rather than resist this process, we feel exhilarated, engaged, alive, and empowered. We have the sensation that we are becoming more than we've ever been. We see possibility everywhere, and we feel blessed beyond measure because we are one of the lucky souls that were given this life experience.

*Contrasting experiences accelerate our evolution,
and when we embrace rather than resist this process, we feel
exhilarated, engaged, alive, and empowered.*

At every moment, and with every thought and emotion we offer, we are breathing life into one of two realities: a reality that we dread, or a reality that we desire. Contrast is a powerful invitation to believe in ourselves and to keep working toward our success, even in the absence of tangible evidence that we will in fact succeed. It is to live with the certainty that when we lose our footing (and we will), we will find it once again. Having it all is holding the image of a giant, blossoming tree firmly in our minds even as we press its fragile little seed into the soil. It's having faith in what is still invisible to everyone around us, while knowing in our hearts that we are right this moment in the process of manifesting it into being.

— • —

PLAY SHEET FOR CHAPTER 7:
Transforming Contrast into Clarity –
The Secret to Having It All

Bring to mind some specific situation in your life that you'd like to be different, or that you have actively been working to change.

As you reflect on this area of your life as it currently exists, allow yourself to see and feel all the ways in which it is not reflective of you having it all. What are the elements of this situation that you most want to change? What people, circumstances or dynamics do you see as the primary obstacles to you having this area of your life look and feel the way you would like it to be?

As you feel the point of tension created by the contrast between where you are and where you would like to be in relation to this subject, allow yourself to acknowledge the clarity that is born from it. What is it that you *do* want to experience in this area of your life? Identify both the material changes you desire to make ("I want a bigger house.") as well as the immaterial ("I want to feel free.").

Allow yourself to see the ways in which the contrast you are now experiencing is acting as fuel to bring you closer to having it all in this aspect of your life. What awareness, understanding or appreciation do you now possess as a direct result of living this contrast? If you allowed it to, what are some ways in which this situation could serve you and bring you closer to what you desire?

Acknowledge that regardless of how it appears, you do in fact have options in this situation, and challenge yourself to make a list of at least nine. Then, reflecting on each of these options, identify the one that carries with it the strongest vibration of empowerment and freedom.

Remind yourself that every situation is made up of two polarities – that which is wanted and that which is not wanted – and you are the one who has the power to decide on which end of this spectrum you place your focus. Choose to use this contrast the way the universe intended – to conjure within you the feeling of your desire already being fulfilled.

CONCLUSION

I once heard it said that for every soul that takes a body, there are a thousand more that desire the experience. Think about this for a moment: You're already here. You got the job! You have nothing to prove, and there is nothing you need to strive to become. The mere fact that you are an embodied being living in this universe that is abundant in all ways, spiritual and material, is in itself evidence that you are deserving of creating and receiving every conceivable manifestation of that abundance. You are the one with the power to mold each piece of your life experience into the shape of your choosing, and when the particular form of something no longer serves or inspires you, you have the power to rework it into a new form that does.

To embrace rather than repress or deny the evolution of our desires is to accept that life was never meant to stand still, and that there is no final destination. Life is a process of continual expansion, and as living, growing beings, we are inseparable from that expansion. We will never be "done" with creating, because creating is what we came here to do. There will never come a time when we are done sorting through the contrast of our experience and using it to clarify our next new direction. Sometimes all we desire is a slight course correction; at other times, a complete 180.

We are always in a transition in some aspect of our lives – just like the old saying goes, "Change is the only constant." Having it all does not mean achieving some once-and-for-all perfect ideal which we are forever obliged to live up to. Our ideas of *it* and *all* will continue to change as we do. It's our ability to *feel* the changes that originate from within us and from outside of us, and to align our beliefs, perceptions, choices and actions with what we desire in each changing moment and circumstance that determines the lives we create.

The experience of having it all will of course include manifesting things we desire on a material level, but key to remember is that what we are truly seeking through their creation is the feeling of exhilaration, accomplishment and freedom we experience each and every time we grow into a larger and more complete manifestation of ourselves. The yearning to experience more of anything in life is born within us for one reason: because we are longing to experience a deeper connection within ourselves.

When we are clutching and searching outside ourselves for contentment, fulfillment, validation or peace, we are not connected to ourselves. When we're feeling out of control with behaviors such as taking things too personally, yelling at our kids, or eating or drinking too much, we are not connected to ourselves. In any area of our lives where we are struggling, feeling confined, or can't seem to make things work, we are not connected to ourselves.

What does it mean to be connected to ourselves? It's being in the presence of the fullness of who we are. It's having access to the 4 percent of us that is focused in this time and space as a material being, as well as the 96 percent of us that is formless and unbounded. It is being grounded in the certainty that we matter; that we have value and worth; that there is no one else like us; and that not only do we belong, but it is also our divine right and responsibility to claim our place as the amazing deliberate creators that we were born to be.

To have it all is to live in the fullness of all that you *already* are. It is to be energetically connected to the truth of who you are, which is complete, full and amazing. The full, expanded experience of who you are cannot be described with words nor conceived with the mind. It can only be experienced through feeling. How connected or disconnected we are to our feelings determines our experience of fullness or emptiness. The feeling is always the key to the fullness – nothing more. Every moment we choose not to feel, we are choosing to not have it all. And every time we say "yes" to our feelings (and therefore "yes" to ourselves), we are choosing to allow the fullness of our being to be expressed. So if you want to have it all, all you need to do is become willing to feel it all – good, bad or indifferent. Only the mind holds us apart. The free-flowing acceptance, awareness and expression of yourself is all that's required. And when there are kinks in the hose (aka *resistance*) that keep you from experiencing the full magnificence of your greatness in any area, know that the key to releasing them comes from the inside.

Behind the world of form, and far deeper than any craving for the things that you have been conditioned to believe will make you happy, is the unseen world where what you are seeking is also seeking you. To invite and allow this unseen world to manifest into your physical experience is to forever alter your concept of who you are and what you are capable of. It is to broaden, change, enliven and expand the inner as well as the outer landscape of your life. To *have it all* is to dare to live audaciously; to experience and express all of who you are in every aspect of your life; to continually be willing to embrace your next evolutionary edge, and the next one after that. It is the commitment to "do" life on your own terms, in your own timing, and in a way that honors your core essence, as it is seeking right now to be expressed.

You and I were born into a universe that is continually expanding, and where our hearts' desires naturally inspire us to expand right along with it. This is like having an "E" ticket to the most amazing ride on earth. Having it all is a journey that both begins and ends with you, and the only ticket required is one you already possess: clarity about your ever-changing desires and the willingness to allow them to come into being. Desire and resistance; having and wanting; defining and redefining are all part of the creative process, and when you understand the forces that are at work behind every act of creation, you gain the awareness to shape your evolving life story – to write it and to rewrite it – into the greatest comedy, drama, romance or adventure that you could possibly imagine.

— • —

ABOUT THE AUTHOR

Christy Whitman is a *New York Times* bestselling author who has appeared on The Today Show and The Morning Show, and whose work has been featured in *People Magazine, Seventeen, Woman's Day, Hollywood Life,* and *Teen Vogue,* among others. As the CEO and founder of the Quantum Success Coaching Academy, a 12-month Law of Attraction coaching certification program, Christy has helped thousands of people worldwide to achieve their goals through her empowerment seminars, speeches, and coaching sessions and products. Christy's life-changing message reaches over 125,000 people a month, and her work has been promoted by and featured with esteemed authors and luminaries such as Marianne Williamson, Dr. Wayne Dyer, Marci Shimoff, Brian Tracy, Neale Donald Walsch, Abraham-Hicks, and Louise Hay. She currently lives in Montreal with her husband, Frederic, and their two boys, Alexander and Maxim.

Meet her at www.ChristyWhitman.com and www.TheArtofHavingItAll.com.